Phonics,
Naturally

Phonics, Naturally

Reading & Writing for Real Purposes

Robin Campbell

HEINEMANN
Portsmouth, NH

Heinemann
A division of Reed Elsevier Inc.
361 Hanover Street
Portsmouth, NH 03801–3912
www.heinemann.com

Offices and agents throughout the world

The author and publisher wish to thank those who have generously given permission to reprint borrowed material:

Figures 1–2, 1–3, 4–1, 6–3, and 6–5: from *Literacy from Home to School: Reading with Alice* by Robin Campbell. Copyright © 1999 by Robin Campbell. Published by Trentham Books. Reprinted by permission.

Figure 2–2: from *Read-Alouds With Young Children* by Robin Campbell. Copyright © 2001 by the International Reading Association. Published by the International Reading Association. Reprinted by permission.

Figure 6–6: from *Literacy in Nursery Education* by Robin Campbell. Copyright © 1996 by Robin Campbell. Published by Trentham Books. Reprinted by permission.

Figure 8–1: from "Literacy Learning at Home and at School" by Robin Campbell, originally published in *Looking at Early Years Education and Care* edited by R. Drury, L. Miller, and R. Campbell. Copyright © 2000 by R. Drury, L. Miller, and R. Campbell. Published by David Fulton Publishers. Reprinted by permission.

Library of Congress Cataloging-in-Publication Data
Campbell, Robin, 1937–
Phonics, naturally : reading & writing for real purposes / Robin Campbell.
    p. cm.
  ISBN 0-325-00709-8 (alk. paper)
  1. Reading—Phonetic method. 2. Reading (Early childhood). 3. Language arts (Early childhood). I. Title.

LB1050.34.C36 2004
372.46'5—dc22   2004005758

Editor: Lois Bridges
Production coordinator: Elizabeth Valway
Production service: nSight
Interior design: Joni Doherty
Composition: nSight
Cover design: Jenny Jensen Greenleaf
Manufacturing: Steve Bernier

Printed in the United States of America on acid-free paper
08 07 06 05 04 VP 1 2 3 4 5

Contents

○ ○ ○

$\mathcal{A}$cknowledgments

o o o

I have been very fortunate in being able to observe many young children learning at home, in preschools, and at school. In particular and recently I have had my knowledge extended as I watched my grandchildren Alice, Caitlin, and Dylan learn to read and write before they started school. I am indebted to them and their parents Robert and Susan for supplying me with so many insights into young children becoming more literate daily. My wife Ruby was often instrumental in demonstrating the links between that learning and the classroom activities that she provided in her preschool and K–2 classrooms. Once again she was the first critical and helpful reader as I produced the chapters of this book. Subsequently, Lois Bridges gave encouragement and help as she moved the manuscript through the process to become a book. I am indebted to them all.

Introduction

○ ○ ○

Some children arrive at preschool or kindergarten with literacy knowledge. They know about books and how they work. They can even read a few words and recite whole books that are familiar to them. These young children make marks, draw and write, and the writing is clearly different from the drawings with letters that are recognizable. Many of them can write their first names confidently and demonstrate knowledge of letters. Their writing contains words that are not spelled accurately but that show they are using their knowledge of phonics. But these children have not yet been to school or been taught directly. How have they learned phonics?

In this book we look at a few children learning literacy at home, and we explore the important literacy activities that those young children have experienced. In particular, we consider how such experiences have enabled them to learn phonics and to do so naturally. Examples of the writing of those children help us to see what they have learned.

But what does that tell us about how we can help all children to read, write, and learn phonics? We explore a number of reading and writing activities in the classroom to note how that supports the children's learning of phonics. Those activities arise naturally out of real reading and writing contexts. They will provide us with clear suggestions of what can be done in the classroom. All of those suggestions are brought together in a final section of the book where "classroom activities to promote learning phonics" are listed to support the busy teacher in the classroom.

Young Children
Making Marks

○ ○ ○

*O*ne morning three-year-old Dylan drew two pictures. He was at home and sitting at a table with a collection of felt pens and some sheets of paper. The first picture he drew was, he announced, a fish (figure 1–1). The second, he indicated, was a shark. The large fin on the back of the shark created a picture different from that of the fish. In addition to the comments about his drawings, however, he indicated that he had written his name. On each picture there were five clear letter-like shapes. And Dylan has five letters in his name.

Of course, it is not possible to recognize his name. But what is evident is the difference between the pictures and the other marks that he said were the writing of his name.

Skillful teachers are aware that when children draw and write, the products offer important information about what the child knows. In this instance, the young child's achievement as he makes the important discrimination between drawing and writing is evident. That achievement is really something special. When it occurs, it shows that the children have learned to represent the world using two modes of representation—drawing and writing. Typically, many children in Western industrialized countries achieve this by about three years of age, that is, before they attend preschool or school. And that important learning to represent the world symbolically by drawing and writing is achieved without direct teaching. Instead, it is the opportunity in the home to make marks, contact with picture books, the experience of seeing writing and pictures in the envi-

Figure 1–1. Dylan's name and fish.

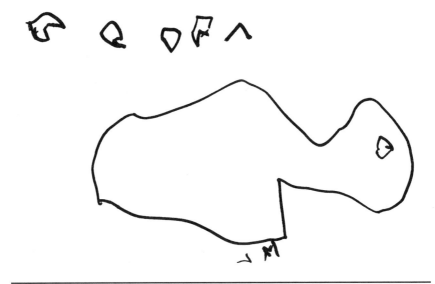

ronment, and support from adults who answer questions and talk about what is seen that enable the children to recognize the distinction between writing and drawing.

A child's drawings and writing enable teachers to analyze what the child has achieved and, therefore, to plan responsive instruction. If we look closely at Dylan's writing, we can detect more than simply five letter-like shapes. In his writing,

1. the numerical representation of his name is accurate with five letter-like shapes;
2. the shapes were written from left to right;
3. the shapes are presented in a horizontal line;
4. the last of the letter shapes is different from the others and has some similarity to the <n> that he will need to write eventually.

Dylan, it seemed, had learned a good deal about the nature of writing. (Notice that here I write the letter name <n>; at other times I refer to a common sound of a letter by enclosing it in parallel lines: /n/. Of course, these are simple and incomplete ways to represent the complex sounds of our language, but it may serve our purposes here. Sandra Wilde [1997] presents a helpful and more thorough representation of sounds that teachers of young children might meet in her book *What's a Schwa Sound Anyway?*)

Prior to producing writing and drawing as separate entities, young children typically produce undifferentiated marks for many months. As they enjoy using pencils, crayons, and felt pens to mark, they often progress to producing large sweeping circular shapes, vertical and horizontal lines, and other marks. Then those drawings become recognizable as representations of objects of interest to the child, perhaps a person or their self-portraits. When children add writing in the form of different types of mark, they have gained a very strong foothold on the web of literacy. As they continue to explore writing, children demonstrate an ever more sophisticated knowledge of writing, reading, and phonics, including such features as letters and alphabet knowledge, phonemic awareness, onset and rime, and letter-sound relationships. All of that is demonstrated by many children before they go to school and, again, without direct teaching. We can see that in more detail if we consider one simple piece of writing by Alice.

Looking at some more writing

When Alice was three years and three months old, she would frequently produce five or six sheets of drawings, typically adding what

Figure 1–2. To Granddad (to gd).

she indicated was her name. On one of those occasions, she decided to construct and then send a birthday card to Granddad (Campbell 1999, 76).

On the back of the card, just as on her other drawings, she wrote her name. At that time she appeared to write "Alioo" for *Alice*. The last two letter shapes might have been an attempt to produce the *ce* ending to her name, but the letter formation was as yet incomplete.

Alice had learned something about the convention of sending messages and in particular of sending cards for special occasions. In itself, that is an important piece of learning for a three-year-old. In addition, the three words that Alice had written—"to," "Gd," and "Alioo/Alice"—were of particular interest. Two of the words were not written conventionally; nevertheless, each of the three words suggested considerable literacy learning had already taken place. The writing also demonstrated the value of close observation of what children are doing, or kidwatching. Looked at in careful detail, their products enable us to understand what they know.

What does the writing show?

At the simplest level, an analysis of Alice's three words demonstrated that she

1. had certain knowledge of seven letters of the alphabet:
   t, o, G, d, A, l, i;
2. could recall and represent the seven letters in writing;
3. knew that words were written left to right;
4. produced the words in a horizontal line;

Figure 1–3. "Alice," three years three months.

5. recognized the need to put the letters in a
   particular sequence;
6. demonstrated an awareness of the need to separate one word
   from another.

It was most likely that

7. the word "to" was part of her visual memory.

She had on other occasions written "to" as a single word as she
made marks with chalk on a chalkboard and with pencils on paper.
Then when sharing a book with an adult, she occasionally pointed
to that word and said "that's *to*" (as well as other words such as *and*,
the, etc.) as the adult read.

In Alice's writing "Gd" for *Granddad*, however, it was likely that
other things were happening and that Alice was using other sources
of knowledge. No one in the immediate family had previously witnessed Alice attempting this word. And she did not ask an adult for
assistance. So when writing "Gd" it appeared that Alice

8. used her knowledge of the letters <g> and <d> as well as
   the letter sounds /g/ and /d/ to write "Gd."

As Donald Graves (1983) indicates, "children are able to com-
pose when they know about six consonants" (184). At first, that composition might include just the initial consonant to stand for the
word. Then the initial and final consonant might be written for the
word, as Alice appeared to do on this occasion. Those invented,
developmental, or phonic spellings indicate the child's developing
awareness of phonics and the ability to use that knowledge. It also
indicates that the significant adults in Alice's life accepted and supported her attempts to write on her own.

Alice also wrote her name, in a form that was close to accurate.
Her "Alioo/Alice" contained a number of positive features in addition
to those we have noted already, such as that

9. there were five letters written and there are five letters
   in her name;
10. the first letters <A>, <l>, and <i> are the correct letters and in
    the appropriate sequence;
11. the <oo> has physical similarities to the <ce> that was
    required.

Alice was close to being able to write her name, with appropriate letter formation, unaided. Within three months of producing that writing, Alice was consistently writing her name accurately. From the first representation of her name with a single capital <A> to the writing of her accurate name had taken about six months. But Alice had not yet been to school or preschool. So how was she, and the many other children like her, able to achieve so much?

How was the early writing knowledge developed?

Many children like Alice and Dylan are able to construct their knowledge of writing, reading, and phonics on a base of rich literacy experiences at home. Before their first birthdays, many children have had numerous contacts with picture books. The focus of those interactive read-alouds gradually moves from the pictures to the print with numerous repeated readings that are enjoyable and instructive. Typically, it is the child who requests those repeated readings. Then playing with language, rhymes, and songs occurs naturally in many homes. However, the opportunity to make marks and to draw and write has to be consciously provided, modeled, and talked about. In that environment, the writing of own name is likely to appear. It is encouraged too by seeing writing and pictures in the environment and talking about them. It is apparent that support from adults and possibly siblings is likely to be important, especially as they talk with the child and respond to the child's questions. A number of case studies demonstrate the way in which young children such as Giti (Baghban 1984), Adam (Schickedanz 1990), Zachary (Laminack 1991), Sarah (Martens 1996) and Alice (Campbell 1999) develop as literacy users at home before going to preschool or school.

Of course, not all children arrive at preschool or kindergarten with a wide range of rich literacy experiences that have promoted their learning. It is important, therefore, that the teacher and other adults in classrooms provide literacy experiences for all children. Among the important classroom activities are

- interactive read-alouds, much more frequently than once a day;
- repeat readings of books to give children ownership of the text;

- shared reading where the children can see the print (big print in the classroom);
- other contact, individually and in small groups, with picture books;
- opportunities for the children to respond to the read-alouds with play, drawing, mark making, and writing;
- play areas for the children to imagine, play, talk, and engage with print;
- singing songs and rhymes;
- other opportunities to draw, paint, mark make, and write;
- opportunities to see own name and to attempt to write it;
- shared writing of lists, notices, and other texts;
- talking about print in the environment and in the classroom.

As we have seen, all of these activities are part of rich literacy experiences at home for many children. The stories from home tell us about the activities that need to occur in the classroom for those who have not had them and for encouraging further the writing, reading, and phonics learning of those who have had such early experiences. In the following chapters, we will look in greater depth first at read-alouds and the activities that extend the children's learning beyond the stories. Then we will explore developments from read-alouds such as shared, guided, and independent reading. Subsequently, we will consider the importance of playing with language, rhymes, and songs; opportunities to draw and write; writing own name; using environmental print; and creating classroom print. In each instance, we will look at how the child at home without direct teaching learns a good deal of phonics from real reading and writing. From that base, in each chapter we will explore in greater detail the activities that might be provided in the classroom to extend that learning. Finally, towards the end of this book, a list of classroom events and activities that have supported the phonics learning is provided.

Read-Alouds
and Beyond

○ ○ ○

*M*any children are fortunate to have contact with picture books from an early age. And as Dorothy Butler (1998) reminds us, contact with books and an interested adult to share the text and pictures are important forces for learning, including literacy learning. At home, that contact might start with conversations with an adult where a book is the focus of the interaction. For instance, when a father was reading a book with his four-month-old, the conversation proceeded like this:

FATHER   Look there's the rabbit.
         Can you see his big ears?
         I think he's going to eat that carrot.
         Let's see what's on the next page shall we?
         What's this a picture of?

Although there is no evidence of the child taking part in this conversation or of reading and commenting on the pictures, everything about the language (and the intonation of the adult) shows an expectation of a key role for the four-month-old child. It was an interactive read-aloud, although the contribution from the four-month-old child was limited to facial responses and body movements.

First, the father pointed to the rabbit and named it for the child. Then he asked a question and, although at this age the child couldn't respond to that question, there was already a suggestion of the reading being interactive with the expectation of a response from the child. Then the father made a suggestion, "I think he's going to eat that carrot," so that prediction is already part of the reading process. The second question asked about turning to the next page and we can note that the language of literacy, such as *page*, *next*, and subsequently *picture*, was part of the interaction.

Of course, we don't know for sure what the four-month-old will have learned from this interactive read-aloud. But we might predict positive outcomes for the child as a literacy learner. That is especially true because, it would appear, the child will over time have an increasingly more vocal role in the read-aloud. It is not difficult to anticipate that the learning will be substantial because this might be one of many thousands of interactive read-alouds that will occur in the home before this child enters a classroom.

Subsequently, one feature of reading storybooks at home that parents will recognize is the request from the two- or three-year-old child to "read it again." Young children love to have books that they have enjoyed read again. Indeed, many parents will recall vividly being tired at the end of a busy day and hearing this request from the child. But those repeat readings are very important. We can detect from the requests that the child has enjoyed the book. It also might be that the child wishes to gain ownership of the text. They can't yet do that by reading the words, so they need to hear the story frequently in order to know fully what it says.

Some young children memorize complete books and, although they still ask an adult to read it to them, they can take part in the reading alongside the adult or tell the story on their own. When Alice was four years, one month, she enjoyed reading alongside an adult with a favorite Eric Carle (1988) book, *Do You Want to Be My Friend?* A typical "reading" included this exchange:

ALICE The mouse is asking,
"Do you want to be my friend?"
But the horse says, No. It's eating the grass.
[Text: "No," said the brown horse, eating the grass.]

Although it is not a precise reading of the text, Alice's memory of the story allowed her to read/recite each page and to demonstrate her knowledge of the content. We are able to observe a comparable occurrence when we watch a young child who is not yet able to read the words in a book, but who has the benefit of many readings, read a book to a favorite doll or toy animal.

Later, as the child tells/reads from another story, some connections are made between words that are recognized in this book and words that are known from other texts. The child demonstrates recognition of some words that have become part of his or her visual memory:

CHILD   That's "do."
              You know, like in "Do you want to be my friend?"

So here four-year-old Alice made a connection between a word she recognized and the story that she had enjoyed many times. Making such a connection indicates that the child is looking closely at the sequence of letters in certain words, recognizing those letters, and reading a word. It also reminds us of some of the literacy learning that takes place from read-alouds.

There are other times when we are likely to notice young children demonstrating their awareness of letters and sounds. For instance, they note words in print that start with the same letter as the first letter in their name:

CHILD   That starts with <a> just like my name.
              But it's not my name.
              I think it says apple.

In this simple example, the child recognized the letter <a>, linked the letter to her name, and suggested the correct word, which also starts with the letter <a> and the same /a/ sound.

So, as we have seen, young children can begin to learn about books, how to use them, and, very important, to enjoy them. They also begin to read or recite books and recognize and learn some words. They learn about phonics, in a number of ways, and letter recognition and application. All of this learning occurs when children are given opportunities to engage with read-alouds and to talk about books that interest them.

Of course, the read-aloud does far more than simply help children to learn letters and words. The read-aloud develops the relationship between the adult and child, encourages the child to think in narratives, and teaches him or her about other relationships, emotions, and the wider world. Children learn about story structure, characters, setting, and plot—not because that is taught, but because it is there to be learned as each story is read. Fortunate young children learn a great deal about reading. And they acquire a love of books.

It is not surprising that read-alouds are seen as such an important feature of early childhood education. Many children learn a great deal from them before they start school. Of course, classroom teachers with a larger number of children to deal with have a more difficult task with read-alouds. Nevertheless, they can still replicate those important events in the classroom and, undoubtedly, want to do so for the benefits that the read-alouds bring.

Interactive read-alouds in the classroom

Interactive read-alouds in the classroom teach children about reading and support them in becoming readers. In the ways that we have already noted, they learn about the nature of books and what it is to read. They learn about the simple physical aspects of how to handle books, turn the pages, and read as the teacher models that process. Story structure is understood implicitly as a variety of picture books are read aloud. Read-alouds also introduce a wider vocabulary and extend the children's horizons to a world beyond their own environment. Of course, read-alouds can achieve something of even greater importance—they can motivate children to want to read and become readers for life. However, as Trelease (1995) indicates, it is not enough to think that an unprepared read-aloud is sufficient. The read-aloud requires careful selection of the books to be read, reading the book as a performance, ensuring that the children take part, and recognizing the importance of repeat readings, especially for the younger children (Campbell 2001; Rog 2001).

There are many children's books of high quality, so the initial task for the teacher is to select from that wide range. The available and appropriate books contain many wonderful stories that will capture the minds of the children. The stories will excite them, cause them to reflect, and encourage them to seek similar books. Additionally, for the younger children in preschool and kindergarten, the story language in a number of the selected picture books might have the qualities of repetition, rhyme, and rhythm. The Dr. Seuss books (e.g., *Green Eggs and Ham*) are well-known examples of such books. The repetition is of phrases and sentences, not solely words. The rhyme element links to children's natural interest in nursery rhyme, song, or rap. When both repetition and rhyme are in place, the rhythm of the language dictates the reading. Listen to an adult reading a Dr. Seuss book and it is very likely that you will immediately recognize and accept the rhythm of the reading.

It is important that the teacher bring young children into the reading and encourage them to participate. It then becomes an interactive read-aloud. Bringing children into the read-aloud is relatively easy with books that contain repetition, rhyme, and rhythm. The children quickly pick up on the nature of the language so that as the teacher reads, there is an encouragement to join in, for example, with *Green Eggs and Ham*:

TEACHER   "Would you eat them
           in a box?
           Would you eat them
           with a..."

CHILDREN   fox?

Skillful teachers use a rising intonation to bring the children into the reading. The teacher reads, "Would you eat them with a...?" with a rising intonation, then pauses to give room for the children to take part. As they do, the children are using the rime element "ox" together with a changed onset <f> for <b> to provide, in this case, "fox." All of this helps children to take part in the reading, to behave as readers, and to learn implicitly about onset and rime. In an interactive read-aloud, the children participate in other ways as well.

Young children comment during a reading. They comment on the story, the characters, the pictures, and the setting. With those comments they tell about similar experiences they have had, relate the characters to their lives, tell about having had this book read to them at home, and so on. Such comments indicate that comprehension of the story is part of the well-presented interactive read-aloud. Of course, the difficult task for the teacher is to accept the children's comments, respond to them, and then move the story forward. Many teachers of young children become very skilled at doing just that; they are responsive to the needs of the children yet maintain the impetus of the story read-aloud.

Some classrooms may have a tradition of providing the read-aloud at the end of the school day. In many classrooms, however, the read-aloud is used near the start of the day because the teacher knows it provides a stimulus for a great number of activities, which we will consider shortly. Some teachers, recalling the importance of repeat readings for young children's literacy development, use read-alouds at both the start and the end of the day. They may also repeat the reading of a story at other times during the day. The teacher who is reflective about classroom activities knows from the children's responses when the repeated reading has become worn and tired for any particular book. Using the read-aloud as part of other curriculum areas is also welcomed. Many interesting and enjoyable stories have useful links to other curriculum subjects. A simple example is *The Very Hungry Caterpillar* (Carle 1969). The life cycle of that creature is part of the story line and, for example, can be developed in a science lesson or lead to an exploration of the foods eaten by various animals.

Thus far I have emphasized the reading of picture books, and teachers certainly make prolific use of that genre, but other texts are important too. Poetry and nonfiction, for instance, can form part of the read-alouds. Poetry often excites the children and gives them further insights into the use of onset and rime as they join the teacher during a read-aloud. Children can also learn the different uses of language in nonfiction as they engage in an interactive read-aloud with such books. Eventually, of course, the teacher uses chapter books as a natural extension from picture books as the subject matter is widened, and books by other authors broaden the children's thinking and enjoyment.

Activities beyond the read-aloud

After a read-aloud, the children typically want to talk about aspects of the story and to relive it in various ways. A wide range of literacy activities are possible. They include:

> Making puppets
> Acting parts of the story
> Engaging in other role-play activities
> Drawing
> Painting
> Making models
> Writing
>> Retelling the story
>> Creating a new ending to the story
>> Producing a new story with the same characters
>> Developing the story with different characters
> Creating books

Singing related songs
Using the story to talk about language, including phonics

Often the children suggest the activities; on other occasions, it is the teacher who suggests an activity.

Of course, teachers encourage different activities to create a variety of possibilities for the children. For instance, in a grade 1 class the teacher read the story of *Sniff-Snuff-Snap* (Dodd 1995). She then invited the children to think of other words to describe the warthog in the story. *Snort* was one of the first words offered, so the teacher added to the task by asking for more words, but only those beginning with *sn-*. As the children provided words (and nonwords that nevertheless seemed right for the warthog), the teacher suggested that they create a new cover for the book and a new title consisting of three appropriate *sn-* words.

Figure 2–1 shows just one of many covers the children produced for their book titles, in this case *Snitch Snatch Sneer*. For the children the task was exciting and creative and developed a sense of authorship—it was a writing activity that seemed authentic. Yet it was also an activity that encouraged phonics learning, as the children considered aspects of letter-sound relationships while thinking about words beginning with the *sn-* consonant blend. And it sur-

Figure 2–1. Cover for *Snitch Snatch Sneer*, a book title created by a grade 1 child following a read-aloud of *Sniff-Snuff-Snap*.

prised the teacher, and me, just how many *sn-* words can be gener-ated that might be linked appropriately to a warthog!

I have written elsewhere about a kindergarten classroom (Campbell 2001) where the children greatly enjoyed a read-aloud. There it was the ever-popular Eric Carle (1969) book, *The Very Hungry Caterpillar*, and the children joined in the reading and made comments. Subsequently, they made puppets, which were used in class retellings of the story. An interesting feature of such retellings is the way in which the shyest children become bold enough to take part and speak to an audience when they stand behind their stick puppet of a caterpillar, four strawberries, or other features of the story.

The children also drew pictures and attempted some writing. Some of the children talked about what the caterpillar ate. Then they extended that to considering what other animals eat. Inevitably, that led to drawing or painting pictures of those animals, then writing to indicate what the animal liked to eat. One of the children, who was not yet five years old, produced some writing under a picture with each of the letters written as a capital letter, "CABET FS" (figure 2–2).

It is not immediately easy to decipher the writing. The lack of a space after "CAB," although there is space before "FS," makes it somewhat difficult to recognize that there are three words in the writing. However, once the writing is deciphered then the more important knowledge that the young kindergarten child demon-strated can be determined. The child

1. recognized that print conveys meaning;
2. wrote in a horizontal line;
3. demonstrated a partial knowledge of space between words;
4. knew seven letters of the alphabet: C, A, B, E, T, F, S;
5. could recall and write seven letters of the alphabet
   in upper case.

So the child gave evidence of some letter knowledge. Beyond that, however, was some evidence of a more sophisticated letter-sound knowledge. The child

6. used the appropriate first letter for each word;
7. had the last letter correct for two of the three words;

Figure 2–2. "Crab eats fish," rendered by a four-year-old as part of a follow-up activity to a read-aloud of *The Very Hungry Caterpillar.*

8. included a vowel A, as well as the initial and final consonant in "crab";
9. produced/invented phonic spellings that approximated the actual sound of each word;
10. demonstrated some phonemic awareness as invented spellings were produced with most phonemes in place.

The child had worked very hard to produce the seven letters. However, when we look beyond the surface features of the seven letters to what the child needed to do in order to produce the writing, then the extent of the achievement is more easily recognized. This example provides a simple but clear demonstration of the reading, writing, and phonics link that can be made in the classroom. After a reading had taken place and when the child engaged with writing unaided, then the child's underlying and developing knowledge of letters and sounds was made evident.

When children are older and more able to sustain their writing, other opportunities are available for the children and teacher to explore. For instance, in a grade 2 class the children had enjoyed a reading of *Hairy Maclary from Donaldson's Dairy* (Dodd 1983), a book that makes considerable use of onset and rime features. And as Moustafa (1997) argues, onset and rime are powerful means of helping children to remember letter-sound correspondences. A simple test of the power of onset and rime can be witnessed when a teacher reads such a story to a class for the first time. The first page has the Maclary and Dairy rhyme, then on the second page another dog is introduced:

> and Hercules Morse
> as big as a ...

If the teacher uses a rising intonation as an invitation to join in, then pauses after "a," very young children, including this grade 2 class, immediately recognize and provide the next word, "horse." They know about rhymes and language structure, so they are able to change the onset letter from <m> to <h> to provide the word and help the teacher continue the reading. The teacher's simple strategy to get the children to provide a word encourages an interactive read-aloud, ensures the children's involvement, and gets the children thinking about onset and rime features in certain words.

Encouraging the children to write similar stories using simple rhyme structures can extend that involvement. One seven-year-old followed the Hairy Maclary story by writing about Samuel Spaniel (figure 2–3). She did so in her self-made origami book, which can be so useful to use with young children (Johnson 1995).

Young children enjoy writing in the context of an origami book because the size of the book appears to make the writing more manageable. It is, as Regie Routman (1991) agrees, "a fantastic and favorite resource that students are able to put together on their own from grade 1 upward" (90), and she demonstrates how the one sheet of paper is folded into an eight-page book (91).

In our example, the seven-year-old child, rather than introduce a number of dogs as the Hairy Maclary book does, recounts the story of one dog, Samuel Spaniel, as he takes his daily walk. In the first two pages of her six-page story, we can see how the seven-year-old makes good use of onset and rime. And we can see how she was able to reflect the Hairy Maclary rhythms in her writing:

> Samuel Spaniel
> his coat is mud brown,
> he loves the country
> but hates the town.

Figure 2–3. *Samuel Spaniel,* an origami book written by a seven-year-old child after a read-aloud of *Hairy Maclary from Donaldson's Dairy.*

Samuel Spaniel
His coat is mad brown,
He loves the Country
But hates the town.

Samuel Spaniel
Loves big trees,
He watches out
for Bumble Bees.

Samuel Spaniel
loves big trees,
he watches out
for Bumble Bees.

When this story was read aloud to the class, the teacher paused before the last word on each page. The children were immediately able to provide that word as the teacher paused before "town" and "Bees." In this example, the young author was able to make good use of onset and rime and the rest of the class was able to recognize the nature of her writing and to provide those rhyming words in the interactive read-aloud. So, in this instance, there were enjoyable read-alouds of the book, writing by the children that replicated the structure and tone of the book, and read-alouds of the children's books. And throughout all of that, the children were learning more about writing and reading and making extensive use of onset and rime.

Careful thinking about words is even more apparent when children write other forms of poetry. In haiku poetry the demand for three lines of five, seven, and five syllables requires children to think carefully about letters and sounds as they consider the syllables in words. In a grade 3 class the teacher read aloud the book, Cimru the Seal (Radcliffe 1996). Following that reading, the children produced writing in a number of genres including narrative, informative writing, and haiku poetry as part of an origami book that each child constructed.

In figure 2–4 we see one child's response with two haiku poems about seals. Although the children were asked to write only one haiku, many produced more than one. These two poems show a clear understanding of the syllabic demands of haiku:

Seals eat crabs and fish
While they're roaming through the sea
Hunting for their prey

Into the attack
Killer whales roam through the sea
Hunting for their prey

The second haiku also shows sensitivity that links well with the nature of the story that had been read aloud. It is interesting to note how competent even young children can become in writing haiku.

Figure 2–4. "Seals," haiku poetry by a grade 3 student.

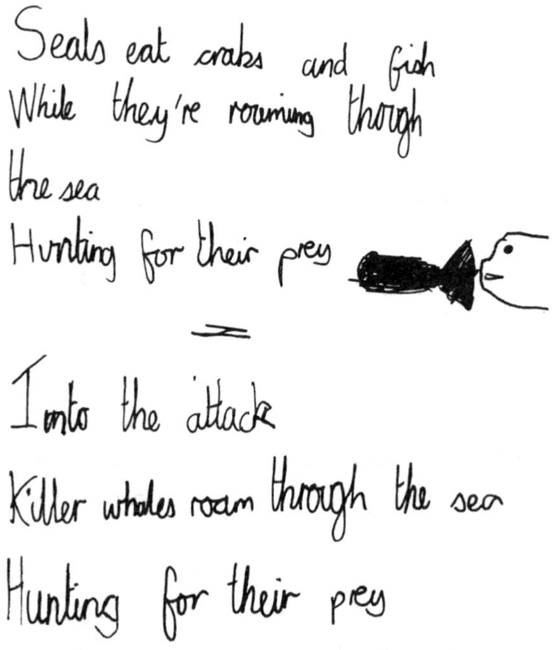

Seals eat crabs and fish
While they're roaming throgh
the sea
Hunting for their prey

Into the attack
Killer whales roam through the sea
Hunting for their prey

And throughout that creative and enjoyable task, the children are engaged constantly in manipulating syllables and, therefore, learning more about letters and sounds.

In summary, the read-aloud is an enjoyable and important part of the school day. In many classes with younger children, it occurs more frequently than just once a day. The teacher has a number of read-alouds because of the enjoyment and benefits that they bring. As we have seen, the read-aloud leads naturally and easily to writing and other reading. It also links the children's involvement with letter/alphabet knowledge, phonemic awareness, onset and rime, and letter-sound relationships.

Classroom read-alouds are different from read-alouds at home, however. They are different in particular because the children in the classroom cannot see the print on the page so easily. At home the child sits alongside an adult and sees the print and selects information from that print to suit current interests and needs. That incidental engagement with the print is less likely to occur in the classroom read-aloud. For this reason, shared reading using big books, guided reading, and independent reading are other very important classroom activities.

Shared, Guided, and
Independent Reading

○ ○ ○

*T*he read-aloud at home changes as the child becomes older. Sometimes it can even seem as though the changes occur daily. The young child who made no verbal contribution during a read-aloud becomes a very vocal contributor as a two- and three-year-old. Memorizing sections of the stories and contributing those during the read-aloud, noting words in the print, and talking about letters are all likely to be apparent. So when Alice was three years old and enjoying a reading of *Good-Night Owl* (Hutchins 1972), she demonstrated some of those attributes. First, she contributed sections of the story from memory:

GRANDFATHER   Owl

ALICE   tried to sleep.

GRANDFATHER   The

ALICE   bees buzzed
               buzz buzz
               and owl tried to sleep.

(Campbell 1999, 70)

Immediately after finishing the story, Alice turned the pages back to the beginning, possibly with the intention of reading the book again. However, her attention was diverted by the bold title pages. On top of each letter of *Good-Night* one of the creatures of the story is standing. On the next line the owl is standing inside the large capital *O*. That led Alice to instigate some comment about the creatures and some of the letters.

ALICE   I think they're all there.

GRANDFATHER   Yes, I think so.

ALICE   Owl's sitting in an <o>.

GRANDFATHER   Yes, and there's some other <o>'s there as well.

ALICE   Squirrel's on one.

GRANDFATHER   And, I think the crows are on another.
                 What else can you see?

ALICE   The sparrow's on a <t>.

GRANDFATHER   Mm.

ALICE   That one is upside down (pointing to the
                 exclamation mark).

GRANDFATHER   It does look like an upside down letter.

ALICE   The robin's going pip, pip.

As that discussion concluded, it was Alice who directed the talk back to the words of the story as she recollected that the robin peeped "pip, pip." Here, too, the three-year-old believed that she recognized the letter <i> but an upside down one when she looked closely at the exclamation mark!

The read-aloud at home becomes very much more than a read-aloud, even an interactive read-aloud, that creates a discussion about or comments on the story. Being close to the print, the child can see and consider the words and the letters within the words, so comments about words or letters can become part of the reading. It becomes a shared reading of the text. It is shared because both adult and child are able to contribute to the reading. And the full content—illustrations, words, and letters—becomes part of that sharing.

As the child develops, the adult's role changes to that of guiding the child through the reading. When Alice was four years and seven months old, she wanted to read a short Paddington Bear book, *Paddington at the Seaside* (Bond 1992). At the start of that reading, Alice immediately started to read but asked for help as soon as she met a word that she was uncertain about:

ALICE	"Paddington at the" What's that word?
GRANDMOTHER	Well, where is Paddington?
ALICE	The seaside.
GRANDMOTHER	That's right; it says "seaside."
ALICE	"seaside Paddington is at the seaside. He //"
GRANDMOTHER	"finds"
ALICE	"finds a //"
GRANDMOTHER	That's a deckchair, like you had on holiday.
ALICE	"deckchair"
GRANDMOTHER	That's it "He finds a deckchair, then"
ALICE	"then goes for a swim."

(Campbell 1999, 108)

During that reading, the adult guided Alice through the text. At times the word was provided for Alice *(finds)*, elsewhere the words were determined by reference to the context *(seaside* and *deckchair)*. However, it was Alice who read and the adult who guided that reading. Such support helps young children to develop as readers and become independent.

Subsequently, the child engages in independent reading. Of course, children do not wait to become proficient readers before they engage in reading events on their own. When children have frequent interactive read-alouds with interesting books at home, they want to repeat those experiences. Then the presence of easily available picture books, on a low shelf, ensures that we will witness very young children engaged in independent reading long before those children are regarded as readers in the conventional sense.

In figure 3–1 ten-month-old Caitlin is investigating the next page of a picture book and doing so on her own. She knew where she could collect a book, and with the aid of the floor as a prop she could intently explore the book independently. At this age, she moves her body substantially to get into a good position to look at the next picture. Nevertheless, she was independently exploring a book. A close observation of the ten-month-old reading tells us that

1. the book was in the correct orientation top to bottom;

2. the pages were turned from front to back;

3. reading-like behaviors were being adopted, including looking at the pages in addition to placing the book and turning the pages.

Many children who are fortunate enough to have books at home and who have had numerous enjoyable interactive read-alouds want to use books on their own. As they do so, they think about the story, look at the illustrations, and wonder about the print. All of this helps them on the exploration to becoming a reader and a mark maker and writer, and it contributes to a developing knowledge of letters and sounds.

The development from read-alouds into other reading activities such as shared, guided, and independent reading occurs also in the classroom. Indeed, during any one school day the teacher may want to organize for each of those four reading activities to take place at

Figure 3–1. Independent reading.

various times. During those activities, the children learn further about reading but also that learning informs their writing and contributes to their understanding of phonics.

Shared reading

It was Don Holdaway (1979) who first described classrooms where big books were used in what he referred to as "shared book experience." Now that literacy activity more frequently is called shared reading. Holdaway started to create and use big books because not all the children in a classroom could see the print during read-alouds. The essential feature of shared reading is the big print, which could "be seen, shared and discussed" (64). Shared reading is an interactive read-aloud with the print—big print—in a position to be seen clearly by the children. When young children have a read-aloud with an adult at home, they can see the print because the book is there directly and closely in front of them. Shared reading attempts to replicate that important part of the experience in the classroom.

Holdaway soon established that not only stories might be made into big print books. Large sheets of paper, or flip charts, constructed with songs and poems in big print were also popular with the children. At that time the big books and sheets of big print that were used were made in the classroom. The substantial numbers of big books now available were not yet published. But the principle was the same: The children could listen to a story, song, or poem and, as they looked at the print, could join in from time-to-time. Among the songs that might be used was the ever popular alphabet song sung to the tune of "Twinkle, Twinkle, Little Star." During repeated singings, the sequence of the alphabet and the letter names are learned. At the same time, because the letters can be seen, letter recognition is encouraged. Singing other songs while looking at the big print contribute to the children's literacy learning in a variety of ways. Key words can be seen and learned, alliterations and rhymes noted, and interesting and unusual words considered, all while engaged in enjoyable singing.

Of course, any shared reading can proceed in a number of ways. For instance, the emphasis can be on the story or on the print. But here I am suggesting that the teachers concentrate on the reading of the story (or song, poem, or other genre). Then on occasion the teacher can use the benefit of the big print to point to the words at the same time. The teacher will know from working with the children in the class how often to point to each word as it is spoken or sung. On a page with few words, the children might be left to follow the words for themselves; with more complex text, greater finger pointing might be appropriate. As the children become more aware of the process, there might be very little pointing by the teacher.

Because it is an interactive shared reading, the children's involvement is an important part of the activity. Occasionally, when the writing has a strong rhyme element, the children are encouraged to join in right from the first reading. As we saw during the classroom read-aloud when the children so easily provided the word *fox* to rhyme with *box*, children will eagerly take part in a shared reading.

TEACHER   "Would you eat them
in a box?
Would you eat them
with a ..."

CHILDREN fox?

But now the children have the added advantage of seeing the word as well as being able to tell it. That being the case, the teacher might briefly attend to the word and talk about it with the children after the story has been read once or twice. Regie Routman (1991) suggests that only on the third, fourth, or fifth reading might some teaching strategies be adopted. On a very few occasions, the teacher might talk about the word at the point that it is read; however, it is typically more appropriate to leave the discussion until after the story has been completed so as not to stop the flow of the story.

In our example, there are a number of ways that a skilled teacher might talk with the children about *fox* and *box*. Upon returning to that page, there might be a consideration of the rime unit, or phonogram, /ox/, and linking by analogy to the few other /ox/ words. Once the teacher does so, it is almost certain that *sox* will be provided, which might be written instead as *socks*. Then there are interesting comparisons to be made between /ox/ and /ocks/ words. The teacher will determine the extent to which those comparisons are made according to the apparent needs of the children being taught. However, making a list of /ox/ and /ocks/ words might occur in the classroom. Or *fox* and *box* might be added to the word wall in the classroom. But the experience with the book comes first and is predominant. The attention to words follows and is secondary.

With younger children, the teacher might emphasize just the first letter of *fox*. From there it is easy to make connections, to ask if there are children in the class who have at the start of their name the letter <f>, using the letter name, or the sound /f/, or both. That question can be extended to ask if any children have an <f> somewhere in their name. Numerous other connections can be made, such as making a list of animals that begin with the same letter or recalling other characters from books that start with an <f>. More simply, the teacher might just ask the children to name other words that they know start with <f>. All of this active learning is derived from the enjoyment of a book and thinking about a character in the story, and it takes up just a small proportion of the time allotted for the shared reading.

However, rather than look in detail at words, on other occasions the teacher might repeat the reading with the children. And with each reading, the children contribute more words. As they do at home, the repeated readings at school have an important place in the reading process. Those repeated readings enable young children to gain ownership of the story. They hear the story, memorize parts of it, or with some books all of it, but still want to hear the adult read it again. Furthermore, during the repeated readings the children note the big print and then learn some of the words. Typically, it comes about quite naturally as children comment on words that they recognize. The teacher then is able to use that comment to talk with the children about these and other words, as well as letters in the words that they might recognize.

Guided reading

At home Alice was able to read *Paddington at the Seaside* (Bond 1992) with the guidance and support of an adult. During that guided reading, the adult provided some of the words, asked Alice to think about the context as a means of determining the word, and generally kept Alice on track as the reader.

In the classroom, the teacher can replicate such support, albeit within a group, during guided reading. The teacher helps readers to develop strategies that can be used subsequently by the children when reading independently. Therefore, as a child is reading, the teacher encourages self-monitoring of the reading such as using context ("Does that make sense in this sentence?") or looking carefully at the words ("What words do you know that start like that?") and looking carefully at letters.

Before supporting the children during the reading, however, the teacher has to organize the children into groups of five or six children with similar interests and abilities. At the start of a guided reading, the teacher introduces a book to the children, during which they will look at the pictures, discuss the features from the illustrations, and perhaps talk about a particular word, or words, from the picture book. For example, when introducing *The Very Lonely Firefly* (Carle 1995) to a group of capable readers, a first-grade teacher first talked about the main character:

TEACHER   Does anyone know what this book is about?

BILLY   A firefly.

TEACHER   It is and can you show me the word *firefly*?

BILLY   There it is, it says *firefly*.

TEACHER   Good, it's a lovely book called *The Very Lonely Firefly*.
I wonder why it's lonely? *(pointing to the word* lonely *as the title is read)*

SALLY   Perhaps no one wants to play.

RICHARD   Or, it might have got lost.

TEACHER   It could be one of those, but it is alone isn't it?

The teacher was able to get one of the children to recognize and point to the word *firefly*. That enabled the teacher to introduce the title, point to the word *lonely*, and begin to discuss with the children why the firefly might be lonely. So a word was introduced and the nature of the story was debated.

The Very Lonely Firefly is a short picture book with a fascinating story line that children can relate to even though it contains some difficult language. The task of reading it is aided by the author's careful use of a repetitive element in the text. On most of the double page spreads there is:

The firefly saw a light
and flew towards it.

But it was not another firefly.
It was a …

The object is clearly illustrated on the double page, so that too aids the young reader. The objects (lightbulb, candle, flashlight, and so on) are lighting, flickering, shining, and so on.

This led the group of children to a discussion about a part of those words, which was instigated by Billy.

BILLY   "But it was not another firefly.
It was a flashlight"
//
It's another –*ing* word.

TEACHER   Well done, Billy.
The flashlight is something in the night?
It does end with –*ing*.

BILLY   "shining in the night."
I know lots of –*ing* words: *eating, talking, running.*

JO   There are hundreds of –*ing* words.

TEACHER   You're right, so –*ing* is a useful ending to look for.

JO   Ending ends in –*ing*.

TEACHER   Yes it does. Now what other –*ing* words were there in this book?

Guided reading provides useful opportunities for the teacher to work with children reading a book. Books can be discussed, words considered, and features of phonics learned; and on occasion that discussion will be led by the children as they note similarities or differences among words. At the same time, the teacher can create a running record of a child's reading to help determine the progress being made. Fountas and Pinnell (1996), in their detailed book, *Guided Reading,* greatly extend those ideas. They also suggest that "the ultimate goal in guided reading is to help children learn how to use independent reading strategies successfully" (2), because, of course, we want the children to become independent readers.

Independent reading

We noted how ten-month-old Caitlin interacted with a book on her own at home. When teachers attempt to replicate such independent reading in the classroom, they need an environment and organization that encourages the children to want to read and then supports them in doing so. Such a teacher working with young children must consider at least three classroom developments that support independent reading: a literacy center, sustained silent reading, and individual reading that includes individual reading conferences with the teacher.

It is important that the teacher create a classroom environment that demonstrates the importance of books. An attractive literacy center can achieve that. Quite simply, the literacy center is set up in a corner of the room so that immediately there are two walls to create part of the boundaries as well as provide the backdrop for displays. A third side, and part of the fourth side, can be enclosed with shelves and book cabinets. Carpeting, soft chairs, and puppets and soft toys of well-known book characters add to the attraction. Of course, it is the selection and display of the books that creates the literacy center. Storybooks, anthologies of nursery rhymes, alphabet books, fairy tales, and information and reference books are all included. For instance, the alphabet books are colorful and attractive but also support the learning of letters and the alphabet sequence. Some books such as *Animalia* (Base 1986) take the learning further as the alliterations for each letter focus on various animals, thereby extending the children's learning. With many interesting books there needs to be space so that a good number of the books can be displayed front-on as an added attraction. Lesley Mandel Morrow (Strickland and Morrow 1989, 2000) describes vividly such literacy centers and suggests a minimum of five to eight books per child to stock the center. Occasionally there might be a display of books about a particular character or by a particular author. Of course, there will be printed materials on display in the center also. (We consider the variety of that classroom print in chapter 8.)

The literacy center is developed because we want children to engage in independent reading. Just as we did for the ten-month-old child who was able to collect the picture books and other texts that were within easy reach on a low shelf, we establish that availability for older children in the classroom's literacy center. The teacher needs to talk about the literacy center and explain the rules: for example, "Only six children in the literacy center at one time please." The teacher, and other adults, might model visiting the center to read a book for a short time. All of that will contribute to the literacy center's functioning well. Then the children will often be seen sitting in the area and reading or looking at books. They will be drawn to take time out, just as they do at home, to read a favorite book or look at another book that is new for them. The well-organized and attractive literacy center encourages young children toward independent reading.

The encouragement of young children toward independent reading can be extended when the classroom is organized to ensure that all the children have a time for reading. After all, it would seem very strange to emphasize the teaching of reading and yet not provide time for children to read. To do so, sustained silent reading (SSR), or with very young children a more reasonable expectation of sustained quiet reading (SQR), is used in many classrooms and schools. In some places a time is set aside when the whole school becomes quiet as all the classes have a quiet reading time. In other schools, the individual classroom teacher organizes a time for all the children in the class to spend reading. The easiest and most effective time to designate for reading is a period following one of the natural breaks in the school day.

The children enter a room after a break and are expected to settle immediately with a book and read for their own enjoyment. There is no expectation that the children will report on their reading; this is a time for reading. With the youngest children, this time may be just five minutes or so. That time can be extended as the children move through the elementary school. Furthermore, with the youngest children, the teacher might want to note reading-like behaviors such as looking at the pictures, turning the pages appropriately, and perhaps running a finger under some words. And a variety of terms are used in classrooms to talk about the activity, so we might see SQUIRT (Sustained Quiet UnInterrupted Reading Time), DEAR (Drop Everything And Read), BEAR (BE A Reader), or ERIC (Everyone or Enjoy Reading In Class). Each term tells us about a classroom organized to provide time for the children to read.

Although there is no expectation of reporting on the reading, it can be useful to spend a few minutes reflecting on the reading at the end of the reading time. For instance, when the teacher reads at the same time as the children (and many teachers believe that it is important to do so), at the close the teacher might reflect on their reading experiences by talking about the book, words, or letters/sounds:

TEACHER   Do you remember that book we read about *The Very Lonely Firefly?* Well, I have just read another book by the same author, Eric Carle. This one was called *The Very Quiet Cricket.* I think some of you will enjoy this book that's all about a cricket, a very quiet cricket, that meets a lot of other creatures.

When a teacher makes such comments after the quiet reading time, two outcomes can be expected. First, some children will want to read the book that the teacher has introduced as well as to look for other books by the same author. Second, some children will want to say something about the book that they have just read. Of course, from time to time the teacher can take a different direction in the comments, so we might hear a question about context such as, "Does anyone know anything about crickets?" or "Does anyone know any other words that begin with /cr/ just like *cricket?*" But the sharing at the end of the quiet reading is just a small part of the time devoted to the activity. Most important is the time set aside so the children can read quietly on their own for a sustained period.

When the children are reading individually, the teacher can take the opportunity to listen in to the reading or to have an individual reading conference. The teacher can replicate in the classroom the at-home experience of sharing a book with a parent, grandparent, or sibling who listens to a child read. First, the teacher listens to the reading and later talks with the child about the book that has been read. After all, meaning, interest, and enjoyment are prime considerations. In addition, the teacher can use a running record, which Marie Clay (1985) has demonstrated to be so useful. Or a miscue analysis can be made to note how the child is using knowledge of letters and sounds, as well as sentence structure and meaning, to read the print on the page. Of course, miscue analysis is typically used under stricter conditions than that of the classroom bustle (Goodman et al. 1987). Nevertheless, a teacher with knowledge of miscue analysis is able to listen to a child read and determine informally a good deal about how the child is using the letters and sounds of our language. And that tells us something about the child's knowledge of phonics.

For instance, when Leah read from *Good-Night Owl* (Hutchins 1972) to her teacher in a grade 1 classroom, she miscued in her reading.

LEAH   "The jays screamed,
        ark, ark,

and owl tried to sleep.
The cuckoo croaked (called)."

The miscue of "called" for "croaked" maintained the meaning of the book and provided a verb for a verb. However, the miscue contained even more because Leah maintained the *-ed* ending and provided the first letter and sound in the miscue. That suggested an ability to recognize the letter <c> and to select an appropriate, although not accurate, word starting with that sound in her reading (Campbell 2001, 73). So the teacher's careful classroom observation enables him or her to develop a picture of the child's letter and sound knowledge while listening to the child reading from a book. And the child is constantly developing that knowledge as books are read in the classroom.

Children further their knowledge of reading in a variety of reading activities, including developing an ever more refined understanding of the constituent letters and sounds. That is helped by the teacher who is vigilant in finding the opportunities to talk about letters and sounds and to support the children in learning about them. Of course, there are other times when letters and sounds can be explored in a number of ways. We will now turn our attention to playing with language, rhymes, and songs.

Playing with Language, Rhymes, and Songs

○ ○ ○

*Y*oung children enjoy playing with language. Before starting school, many children experience rhymes of various kinds, including traditional nursery rhymes and more contemporary rap rhymes. They play with songs and sing on their own or with members of their family. Then as they become more aware of letters, they enjoy playing games with language such as "I Spy" and "Hangman." For some children, those early experiences with rhymes provide the basis for subsequent drawing and writing.

Children recite rhymes that are familiar to them. Those recitations may occur quite spontaneously at any time of the day. On one occasion while sitting at the breakfast table and without apparent prompting, three-year-old Caitlin broke into a recitation of a nursery rhyme that she knew. There had been no mention, or singing, of rhymes by anyone at the table. Out of the blue, Caitlin sang:

> One, two, three, four, five,
> once I caught a fish alive.
> Five, six, seven, eight, nine, ten,
> then I let it go again.
> Why did you let it go?
> Because it bit my finger so.
> Which finger did it bite? .
> This little finger on the right.

Caitlin also wiggled the little finger on her right hand at the end of the rhyme (Campbell 1998, 79). Examples such as this tell us how children are thinking about language and rhymes. They enjoy the rhythm and rhyme of nursery songs and other playful language. At the same time, children are learning incidentally about onset and rime; for instance, the first two lines contain the rime unit of "ive" and the initial onset of "f" and "al." Subsequently, there is the more simple onset of "g" and "s" and the rhyme of "o" as the child recites "so" and "go." All of that helps to build the child's understanding of letters and sounds.

Furthermore, as Chukovsky (1963) indicates, many children move beyond memorization and recitation to make up their own rhymes as they play. For instance, he observed his four-year-old son running around the garden while riding an imaginary horse, a broomstick that was readily available, and shouting out at the same time a poem that he had just composed:

> I'm a big, big rider,
> You're smaller than a spider.

(Chukovsky 1963, 64)

Those two lines are similar to the pairs of rhymes that Caitlin sang, but here the child was the composer. Children create their own simple rhymes, with onset and rime in place, especially if they have had considerable experience with a wide range of rhymes and when their play with language is accepted and encouraged by adults.

The involvement with language rhythms starts at even a younger age. For instance, during a car journey when Alice was two years six months old, she started to sing a short rhythm "ba ba ba // ba ba ba." I repeated that rhythm and then suggested a different one by singing "ba ba // ba ba," which Alice immediately copied. Subsequently, I initiated and Alice sang other rhythms such as "bi bi bi // bi bi bi" and then eventually on to "be be be // be be be" and "bo bo bo // bo bo bo." Of course, Alice had to initiate some rhythms for me to follow and so the game and laughter continued. Great fun, but also language learning as Alice listened carefully to the rhythms and phonemic changes that occurred and then uttered them on her own. In some respects, that game reflects the communication that can often occur between an adult and a child at about one year old as the babbles that they produce, such as "da, da" and "ba, ba," are repeated by the adult. The child and adult enjoy it and the child develops a phonological and phonemic awareness.

All of that oral involvement with rhymes and songs can lead in due course to drawing and writing that links to the rhymes. So Alice, when three years three months old, recited "Humpty Dumpty" to her younger sister. She did so as they looked together at a nursery rhyme book. Such episodes are repeated frequently by young children as they return time and time again to the familiar. Eight months later, just before her fourth birthday, Alice returned to that nursery rhyme to draw and write about "Humpty Dumpty sat on the wall" (figure 4–1).

The picture, which was colored with crayons, did resemble Humpty Dumpty. Her writing provided further evidence of Alice's growth in understanding of letters and sounds. For instance, "wll" required only the vowel "a" to complete the spelling of *wall*. The letters that were written are the ones we hear most clearly when we say that word. It is difficult to determine what else was written on this occasion, although the clear *H* does suggest an attempt at the name. All of this was done playfully and Alice was learning phonics, although no direct teaching was taking place.

Of course, young children play other language games. "I Spy" and "Hangman" are two enjoyable language games that encourage young children to think carefully about letters and sounds. One early morning, three-year-old Caitlin and her elder sister Alice joined their grandmother in bed. After brief conversations on a

Figure 4–1. Humpty Dumpty sitting on the wall, rendered by Alice at three years eleven months.

number of topics, Caitlin indicated that she wanted to play "I Spy," a game in which one person provides the first letter or sound of an object that they can see. It was a game that she had listened to her sister play and in which she had taken part on occasions.

CAITLIN	Let's play "I Spy."
GRANDMOTHER	Go on then, you start.
CAITLIN	I spy something beginning with <e>.
ALICE	It's got to be in the room Caitlin.
CAITLIN	Elephant.
GRANDMOTHER	No, it's got to be in the room.
CAITLIN	Okay. I Spy with my little eye something beginning with /cl/.
ALICE	Clock.
CAITLIN	Yes, and another /cl/ for cloth *(pointing to the duvet cover)*.

(Campbell 1998, 78)

Although the game got off to a false start because Caitlin could certainly not see an elephant, nevertheless she did indicate the appropriate first letter <e> for the object she was thinking about. Subsequently, she provided a sound /cl/ for her next word, which was probably *cloth* rather than *clock*, we might guess from her comments. However, not only was the three-year-old learning more about the conventions of this game, she was also thinking about letters and sounds and attempting to deduce the initial phoneme in a word.

Children also enjoy playing the word game "Hangman." (It can be renamed "House," "Window" or other object if required; the aim remains to attempt to complete a word by suggesting letters one at a time and trying to complete the word before any incorrect letters allow the picture to be completed.) At just five years of age, Dylan had learned the game from his older sisters. He liked to choose the word and draw the picture. On one occasion he played with his grandmother (figure 4–2).

We can see that the letters *a, i, e,* and *o* were rejected and led to the construction of four lines of the hangman's gallows. The five prepared spaces for the word were completed eventually with the letters *p, u, d, o,* and *l* because Dylan had decided that was the

Figure 4–2. A game of hangman—puddle.

spelling of *puddle*. Of course, the letter <p> was reversed and the <d> was written as a capital letter, as we might expect from a young child whose name starts with a capital D. The frequent use of a capital letter whenever the first letter of the child's first name is written is not at all unusual. On this occasion the five letters do create a very close approximation to the sounds required for the word *puddle*. It is important that the enjoyable game involved a good deal of thinking about a word, letters, sounds, and spellings. Children can be actively engaged with learning phonics while the apparent focus is an enjoyable game.

Rhymes and songs in the classroom

It is very clear how our understanding of children's learning at home links to the preschool, kindergarten, and grade 1 classrooms. The examples that we have seen demonstrate that it can be very useful for children to learn rhymes, including traditional nursery rhymes, songs, and rap. It is useful because it develops the children's awareness of a cultural heritage. It also aids oral language development, helps them to learn about letters and sounds, and can be a stimulus for reading and writing. Teachers in early years classrooms often use similar activities with the very young children in the classroom.

Learning various rhymes including songs needs to be a regular part of each day. The first reason is that the children love to sing and it adds to their repertoire of known rhymes and songs. Second, it promotes phonemic awareness and informs about aspects of onset and rime as well as other aspects of letters and sounds. Third, that learning and knowledge helps them as they read and write. In addition to rhyming songs, the alphabet song sung to the tune of "Twinkle, Twinkle, Little Star" has its own rhythm and teaches the letter names and alphabet sequence (Strickland 1998). Mills and colleagues (1992) suggest a range of alphabet songs for children to learn too. It requires only a few minutes each day to be set aside for this activity in order for the children to acquire a considerable number of rhymes and songs during a school year.

In addition to setting aside a few minutes for singing, many teachers get the children to recite rhymes or sing songs during transitions from one activity to another to lessen the possible disruptive nature of those transitions.

In some instances singing songs and learning rhymes link to other activities such as the read-aloud. There are picture books where the story line is very specifically that of a song, as in the book *Row, Row, Row Your Boat* (Goodhart 1997):

> Row, row, row your boat
> Gently down the stream,
> Merrily, merrily, merrily, merrily,
> Life is but a dream.

In such cases, teachers can read or sing the book to the children and gradually get the children to join in until they know all of the verses. There is an extensive and helpful list of rhyming texts provided by Opitz (2000) in his book *Rhymes and Reasons*. Many of those texts are picture books that contain a good deal of onset and rime as we noted earlier in some of the books written, for instance, by Dr. Seuss (e.g., *Green Eggs and Ham*) and Lynley Dodd (e.g., *Hairy Maclary from Donaldson's Dairy*).

In another book, *Slinki Malinki*, by Lynley Dodd (1990), the structure and rhyme is very similar to *Row, Row, Row Your Boat* when we read about the cat Slinki Malinki:

> He was cheeky and cheerful,
> friendly and fun.

He'd chase after leaves
and he'd roll in the sun.

Young children greatly enjoy the adventures of this cheeky cat. The children can relate to the cat's antics. The story line provides great enjoyment as well as telling about relationships and behavior. Of course, there is also the onset and rime. So the read-alouds of this and many other picture books provide close links to the rhymes and songs that children have heard and enjoyed and from which they learn phonics. The similar structure of the texts also helps give the children an expectation of the writing, which helps them to predict words when they read similar books.

Of course, as well as hearing the rhymes and perhaps seeing the print in big books or other very visible print such as large print on big sheets or whiteboard, the children can benefit from seeing the rhymes being written. In one preschool classroom the teacher encouraged the children to join in and support the writing in big print onto a large sheet of paper:

TEACHER So if I write
"Humpty Dumpty"
Now, what comes next?

CHILDREN sat on a wall

TEACHER I'll write
"sat on a ..." (?)

CHILDREN wall

TEACHER wall.

So the involvement with a nursery rhyme can be linked into a shared writing of the known text. And the teacher can ask for even greater help because prior to writing "wall" she asked:

TEACHER Who can help me with *wall*?
What letter do I need to start?

WENDY /w/

TEACHER Yes, it is a /w/.
I think it is like your name, isn't it, Wendy?
It starts with a /w/.

Eventually the nursery rhyme is written completely and can then be used as the basis for a shared reading of the rhyme by the class. If the children draw some pictures to cut and paste around the text, then a feeling of authorship and ownership adds to their interest in reading the print with the adult.

At other times the teacher might, during a shared writing of the rhyme, have the children write some of the letters or words. So the children "share the pen" as McCarrier, Pinnell, and Fountas (2000) argue in their book, *Interactive Writing.* Therefore, in our previous example there would be a change in the contribution from the children:

TEACHER   Who can help me with *wall?*
What letter do I need to start?

WENDY   /w/

TEACHER   Yes, it is a /w/.
I think it is like your name, isn't it, Wendy?
It starts with a /w/.
Who can write the /w/ for us?

JOHN   I can.

TEACHER   Come on then, John, you write the /w/.

Now the activity is serving a different purpose. The written text might not be bold and clear enough to be used in a subsequent shared reading with the whole class. It has served other purposes, however. It required the children to think carefully about the words in the rhyme. They also have thought about the sounds, or phonemes, that they can recognize in those words to then produce as print. And the children who contribute to the writing gain confidence about their ability as writers. During this activity reading, writing, and phonics learning are linked in an obvious way as the children work with the teacher on the task.

Language games

There are numerous enjoyable language games that children like to play. And those games encourage them to think about words, letters, and sounds. The learning is part of the enjoyable activity rather than seeming to be taught directly. We have noted already that children at home, once they know about such games, will often instigate the playing of them. In the classroom, the teacher can use that interest to organize the games as class, group, or paired activities.

In a number of preschool classrooms I have seen children individually and as a class clapping out the syllables in their own first names. Sometimes that game is linked to a short time spent singing rhymes and songs. In some cases, the teachers even found that it was possible for the children to clap the syllables in the rhymes and songs. What the simple name-clapping activity does is to encourage each child to think about his or her name and how it sounds. And young children seem to be able to pick out the syllables in words very quickly. The three-year-olds that I have observed were able to clap out the syllables in their names and the names of their friends without fault. Being able to do that at a young age meant that the children had the basis for understanding onset and rime and much later producing syllabic poetry such as haiku.

The language game "I Spy" is best organized as a brief class or group activity. Once again the game encourages the children to think about a word and the letters and sounds of it. In particular, they have to attempt to deduce the initial phoneme in the word so that they can say, for instance, "I'm thinking of a word that begins with /b/" as they look at the books in the literacy center. The activity supports phonemic awareness learning in a fun way. All the children are involved because each child is looking around the room for an object that begins with the /b/ sound. When this is a class activity, the teacher can add to it by writing the children's suggestions in big print in front of them. Typically, we would expect to see an ever growing list of words beginning with /b/. There might also be a smaller list of ad hoc words beginning with other letters so that the teacher can ask the children why they are not likely to be correct. Of course, the /b/ list of words can lead to another game—how long can we make this list using only objects beginning with /b/ that we can see in the classroom?

The word game "Hangman" might be started as a class activity as a simple way to ensure that the children understand how to play the game as the teacher models the process in front of the children. We have seen how a five-year-old at home learned the game very largely from observing his older sisters playing it. In the classroom, the children can quickly learn the rules as they provide a letter and see it put into place or rejected. They then might move to a more sophisticated understanding of how to play. With guidance grade 1 children can very quickly begin to see that randomly providing letters is not very helpful. Do we need a vowel in this word? What letters occur more frequently in words? Such questions might be asked initially by the teacher but subsequently by the children as they try to solve the word puzzle. Subsequently, children might play the game in pairs. In each instance, the children are thinking about words, letters, sounds, and spellings.

Children can have fun thinking about and writing alliteration. In a grade 1 classroom the teacher had read aloud the big book *Walking through the Jungle* (Lacome 1993). Following that reading and after discussing alliterations, each child wrote an alliteration about an animal (Campbell 2001). A few of the children chose the flamingo, although not featured in the book, as the featured creature when they wrote alliterations (figure 4–3).

In this example, the child produced alliteration that had the /fl/ sound at the beginning of four of the words. So "A fluffy flimingo flying flapping its wings," although it contained a misspelling of *flamingo*, had a good flow of language. To produce such writing, the children had to select from some known words and think carefully of letters and sounds. All that was done in the context of responding with interest to a read-aloud. There are, of course, books that demonstrate the use of alliteration in a very substantial way. Margaret Atwood's (1995) book *Princess Prunella and the Purple Peanut* is enjoyed by somewhat older children for the unique way that the story is told with, as we can see in the title, an alliteration of <p>.

Among the other games that might be played is what Dorothy Strickland (1998, 64) refers to as the "I'm thinking of a word" game. As a class activity the teacher asks the children, for instance, "What word could this be? It begins like *ball* and rhymes with *tack*." Here the emphasis is on onset and rime. First, as with the earlier games,

Figure 4–3. Alliteration about a flamingo, written by a child in grade 1.

A fluffy flimingo flying flapping its wings.

the children can start by providing the word orally. Subsequently, in order to involve all of the children with each word, the children can write the word independently and then share with a partner what has been written. Once again this is a brief activity and linked to words that the children know, perhaps examples taken from some of the picture rhyming books that the children have enjoyed. Furthermore, although the game is emphasizing onset and rime, it is in part also showing children that words can be worked out by analogy. If I know *tack* I can work out *back* and *sack*, *lack*, and *rack*. That phonic knowledge helps the children as they continue to read and write.

5

Opportunities to Draw and Write

○ ○ ○

*W*hen children at home have paper and pencil (or ballpoint, crayon, etc.) available, they appear to be self-motivated to mark make. They want to draw and to write. We noted in chapter 1 that the marks they make initially look very much like undifferentiated scribbles. However, by about the time a child is two years old, the marks begin to take shape and faces, people, animals, and other objects appear in a more recognizable form. Then comes that magical moment when the child produces both drawing and writing. Of course, as we noted with three-year-old Dylan in chapter 1, the writing is not immediately readable. But it is clearly different from the drawing as the child produces letter-like shapes. Subsequently, those shapes begin to look more and more like letters until there are real messages to be read. Of course, for a while the adult has to look carefully and thoughtfully at what is being produced in order to understand the message. As Prisca Martens (1996) demonstrates, when Sarah wrote "ILU" at the end of a thank-you note, each letter represented a word. The message was of course, "I love you." But what was written was logical and governed by rules that Sarah was generating for herself about how written language works. "I" was written appropriately, "L" represented the initial consonant of the word *love* (you may recall Donald Graves [1983] suggests that rule is applied by many children for a while), then in "U" the letter name is the same sound as the word *you*. Teachers who look carefully at the writing of many young children become very accomplished at reading their efforts and noting the rules that the children are using to govern that writing.

Children are helped to generate those rules by the print they see in the environment and in the picture books that they share, together with the support from adults and others who talk about language. For instance, an adult provides a simple example of that support as he or she prepares to go shopping. Often the adult writes a shopping list. In the presence of a young child, it is helpful if the adults talk out loud as the list is written. Young children learn from such modeling as they see the word written and hear it spoken. In addition, the children are intrigued by the process and want to try it themselves (figure 5–1).

The preschool child was helped in this instance by the shape of the paper. Nevertheless, the child produced what looks like a list with both letter-like shapes and a few letters evident. There is the possibility that the word *milk* is contained in the list. The opportunity to write encourages the children to think about words, letters, and sounds. And as they do so, they refine the rules that they are applying, so the spellings that they produce move closer to becoming conventional.

At about the time that she started school, five-year-old Alice produced some writing at home on a folded piece of paper. That meant there were four sides, or pages, for drawing and writing. The front cover of her book was entitled "information book" but written by Alice as "ifmasn book" (Campbell 1999, 131). Although an uncon-

Figure 5–1. Shopping list written by a preschool child.

ventional spelling, it demonstrated her willingness to attempt to write a long and complex word using her knowledge of letters and more particularly the sounds. As we read her attempt at the word, we can detect how she managed to produce that particular spelling. Inside the booklet on one of the pages she wrote about snails (figure 5–2).

On the page about snails she wrote:

sayl
sayls hav
he shl on is dak

One of the most interesting features of this writing is the way in which it was set out. There is a heading "snail" before some information is provided about that creature.

snail
snails have
he(the) shell on its(his) back

Alice had learned about information books and how they are set out because they were among the books that she liked to look at and to read. In her booklet she was replicating the organization of those books. Her reading of a variety of books enabled her to structure her own writing.

Figure 5–2. An information book about snails written by five-year-old Alice.

In addition she used her knowledge of phonics, which had been generated by a great deal of reading and writing, to write some information about snails. Although I have presented a conventional interpretation of her writing (with two possible variations), it was probably not necessary to do so as her writing had become close enough to the conventional to be readable. But can a teacher with twenty or more children in the class organize sufficient opportunities for authentic writing so that the children can develop their understanding of phonics there, too?

Opportunities to draw and write in the classroom

We have seen how read-alouds can often act as a stimulus that encourages the child to draw and write. It is one immediate way that we provide opportunities for writing in the classroom. Then the shared writing of nursery rhymes and songs enables a conversation with the children as to how writing is constructed. There are possibilities for writing beyond those important literacy activities.

In a number of preschool and kindergarten classrooms, the children have a wide range of play activities to choose from. Typically that might include an area set aside for imaginative or sociodramatic play. That area or corner could be set up as any of the following:

Post office
Supermarket
Travel agency
Veterinarian's office
Dentist's reception and waiting room
Restaurant

A number of different props can soon transform the area to create the particular environment. But an important addition is literacy materials. So the post office would have these items:

Notices
Instructions
Forms to be completed
Envelopes to be addressed
Telephone and message pad
Typewriters and keyboards or computers.

When such provision is made, three- and four-year-old children explore literacy with interest as an integral part of their imaginative play. They make marks and produce letter-like shapes, letters, and words. That experience is enhanced when the teacher visits the post office and demonstrates the possibilities as part of the play activities. Those demonstrations are just offered as part of the play activity. The teacher does not have to ask the children to watch or listen. Instead, the teacher can just visit the "post office" and speak aloud, for example, "Now let me see. I'll send this birthday card. So I better put the address on the envelope." Children like to replicate the literacy tasks that they see adults completing. When they do so, the children think about letters and sounds to produce the words that they want to write.

A more direct literacy provision in the preschool and kindergarten is a writing center. The organization for that is very simple. It requires a table and perhaps as many as six chairs, a collection of paper (of different sizes, colors, and shapes that can be varied regularly), and a collection of writing implements (pencils, crayons, and felt pens). The children can be encouraged to visit the center as long as there is a vacant chair. A display of writing on an adjacent wall adds to the center. Of course, the teacher needs to visit the center on occasion to model writing, perhaps to write a shopping list just like the parent at home, to talk with the children about their writing, to answer their questions, and to encourage them to write independently. Much of the discussion will be about the important areas of ideas, content, and structure. Part of the discussion here, and with the whole class on other occasions, is to support the children toward conventional spelling.

Sometimes discussions in the writing center become a mini-lesson, in the same way that the children's interaction with the teacher about *-ing* words grew from a guided reading of *The Very Lonely Firefly* (Carle 1995). For a few minutes the teacher and children might be engaging in the following activities:

Listening to the sounds in particular words

Discussing one specific sound found in a number of words

Talking about word endings

Creating a list of words that rhyme

Talking about word beginnings

Thinking of words that help alliteration

Looking carefully at ten key words (*a, and, in, is, it, to, the, that, of, you*) that make up 25 percent of the words when reading

Those and other minilessons occur as a result of the close observations by the teacher, who can then respond to current issues and needs. The minilesson that is based on what the children are writing is a far more powerful lesson than one that is decided in advance.

We have seen how the shared writing of a nursery rhyme can be a useful activity in the classroom as the big print is constructed on a large sheet of paper, whiteboard, or overhead projector. But shared writing is used far more extensively than just the important rhymes. A wide variety of topics for writing can be demonstrated as the teacher writes in front of the class and discusses with them the ideas to develop the writing. Together they might

Retell a familiar story.
Make a new version of a known story.
Make up a new story.
Tell about personal experiences.
Describe an object.
Write letters.
Create birthday, and other, cards.
Record information.
Write instructions.
Make a list.
Develop a recipe.

As these are composed, the children contribute to the writing by their comments and suggestions. They see the writing being constructed. And they begin to create in their own mind ideas for independent writing in the future. In addition to composition and the very important development of ideas is the transcription of shared writing, the actual writing of words and sentences. Then the teacher and class discuss the word to be used, recall the spelling of key words, and consider the spelling of more complex words. At times that involves discussion of the letters and sounds that will help in those spellings. Thus, shared writing encourages phonic learning because the children and the teacher together discuss the words that are used.

The writing together is even more obvious when the shared writing becomes interactive writing (McCarrier, Pinnell, and Fountas 2000). Then the young children "share the pen" and physically do some of the writing. The teacher is still leading the discussion and still discusses both composition and transcription, but now the children do the writing whenever possible. Some of the youngest children might contribute only the first letter of a word. An older child can contribute a key word from memory, or write a more complex word from a discussion of the sounds in the word and the letters that might associate with those sounds. Sharing the pen is important for preschool and kindergarten children when the physical act of writing with adult support is still important. As the children become more competent with their writing, shared writing may be more appropriate.

An important task for the teacher during shared and interactive writing is to maintain an appropriate balance. These literacy activities provide a model of both what to write (composition) and how to write (transcription). Both are important for the children. Therefore, the teacher needs to reflect carefully on the nature of the shared and interactive writings in the classroom in order to maintain the best balance for the children. Of course, these activities are developed to support the children in their independent writing. And teachers should ensure that there is time each day for the children to write on their own.

Much of the initial independent writing produced by young children is likely to be related to experiences. Initially, in a language experience approach, the teacher wrote for the child. That happened as the child dictated his or her experience to the teacher. Now it is recognized widely that the child who can talk about experiences is also able to write about them in some form. That process of writing is a very important part of the child's learning. When children write, they are motivated to work out the spellings of words so that they are thinking about letters and sounds as they produce phonic spellings. For instance, when a kindergarten child produced a reflection of the shopping list that we had seen the preschool child produce, the list was more readable although the spellings were not yet conventional.

The list of seven fruits (figure 5–3) contains one word, *plums*, that is spelled conventionally. The other six words demonstrate a clear use of phonic knowledge and understanding to create the

Figure 5–3. A list of fruits.

invented spellings. Each word had the first letter in place together with other consonants and vowels that closely resemble the sound of the word. Perhaps the most difficult word to read was *tangerine* because the <n> was omitted, a not infrequent occurrence, as Sandra Wilde (1997) reminds us, especially when it precedes a consonant or is linked to <g>. Then the <g> is changed to a <j> and then reversed at the same time, as it is in *orange* farther down on this list. But the word can be read and the child's intentions and thinking exposed. There is a further reversal of the letter <g> in *grapes*. In kindergarten these reversals are still fairly common and are corrected in the main by the children during the course of the year, providing they write and read daily and receive support from the teacher. Reversals need to be noted by the teacher. However, the considerable contacts with and talks about print in the classroom help most children learn what is required. Finally, if we look at *bananas* on this list, we see how very close it was to its conventional spelling. But it was written without the first <a> of the three that are required. It is the most difficult <a> in this word because it is not possible in most dialects to hear clearly which vowel is required. Nevertheless, what this five-year-old achieved in that word and the others in the list was very substantial. Here, as elsewhere in our examples of children's writing, we can see how writing creates a phonic lesson.

Sam produced a quite different piece of writing when he was given the opportunity to write independently. This five-year-old decided to write his own story about pigs (figure 5–4).

Before looking at the words used by the five-year-old, we should note the well-constructed story. Sam is a writer. He has learned many of the conventions of writing. Then he has moved beyond simpler forms of writing to construct an interesting short story. It would appear that he has knowledge of narrative writing that will enable him to progress well with many different genres of writing in the future. However, here we need to look rather more simply at the words that he wrote both conventionally and as phonic spellings. The story has 38 words, some of them repeated, so there are 32 different words written by Sam. Sixteen words are written conventionally:

| a | and | day | get | he | his | in | met |
| mud | of | one | pig | the | them | they | to |

It is likely that some of those words are established firmly as part of his visual memory. Among these words were six (*a, and, in, of, to, the*) of the ten key words that we referred to earlier. Knowledge of

Figure 5–4. Pig story by five-year-old Sam.

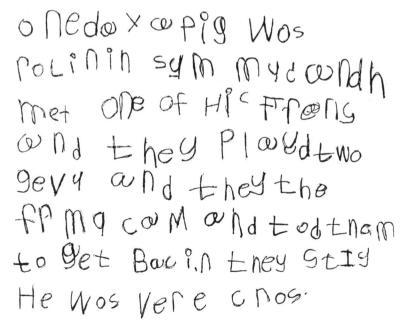

them enables Sam to create a simple structure in his writing. Among the conventionally written words, however, Sam may have written *pig* and *mud* as he thought about the sounds in the words and then wrote the letters to correspond with the sounds. Nevertheless, Sam had a collection of words that he could write accurately and that provided a foundation for other writing.

There were 16 phonic spellings in Sam's writing. One of those, "h" for "he," may simply have been the result of being on the edge of the page and the "e" may have been lost in the process. The writing of "they" for "their" and "then" represents the difficulty that very young children appear to have in discriminating between the numerous "th" words that they meet in reading and writing.

they[their]   they[then]

The other phonic spellings indicate how knowledgeable this five-year-old had become about the letters and sounds in his language. Each word had the appropriate first letter and sound.

Bac	cam	cros	frma	frens	h	playd	rolin
sum	stiy	tod	two	geva	vere	wos	

Additionally, in four of the words he wrote the initial digraph accurately: "cros, frens, playd, stiy." All the words had letters to represent the final phoneme in the word. It was possible to see how Sam had arrived at the letters he wrote for word endings. Nevertheless, "a" for "er"; "d" for "ed"; "in" for "ing"; and "iy" and "e" for "y" suggested that word endings might be a topic for mini-lessons in the classroom alongside more and more opportunities for writing. But we need to remind ourselves of how well this five-year-old was using phonic knowledge. He had the first and final sounds in place and consistently placed a vowel in the appropriate position in each word. The writing of "twogeva" for "together" produced an interesting spelling. However, it was a perfect representation of the spoken word in his dialect. It demonstrated how carefully he was attending to the sounds of each word and then attempting to represent those sounds with letters on the page.

In addition to independent writing, other subject areas across the curriculum provide numerous opportunities for writing. Teachers have the task in the elementary classroom of considering how best to teach the subject and what meaningful reading and writing can be linked to that teaching (e.g., writing observations and reports in science; letters, lists, statements, reports, and reflections in social studies). The list of writing opportunities across the curriculum is substantial. That writing helps the children to learn about the subject as they extend and clarify their thinking. And the writing requires them to think about sounds, letters, words, and sentences in the content being written.

When I was the teacher in an elementary classroom, I attempted to ensure that there were always authentic reasons for writing. Therefore, class projects were organized to study an area in some depth. So, for example, the Roman civilization or the Lewis and Clark Expedition became the focus for reading, writing, art, and discussion. The projects might be designed to last a week, a month, or a term. Sometimes they last longer than expected but others finish earlier than planned. The teacher's close observation of the children's involvement helps to assess the length of the project. As a balance to the class project designed by the teacher, the children had time to explore an individual topic of interest to them. When young children are given such opportunities, the range of topics covered within the class is huge—trees, ships, butterflies, frogs, "When my grandma was young," and so on, will come under the scrutiny of the children and lead to further writing. A strategy to bring together the choices of the children and the planning of the teacher was a one-day theme. First, the children created a list of themes they would like to explore together. Then every two weeks or so a whole day would be designated theme day. The children, many with the help of their parents, would collect books, pictures, and objects related to the theme of the day. Then the children would busy themselves for the day in finding out, reading, writing, drawing, painting, making models, and talking about the theme. It was busy, hectic, and enjoyable. The children had something to write about and did so enthusiastically. Therefore, in that elementary classroom there were class projects, individual topics, and one-day themes all designed to extend the children's thinking and to provide authentic reasons for reading and writing.

Ensuring that the children have numerous opportunities to write is vital. They need to write daily and that writing has to be authentic and meaningful to the children. When they engage in that writing with a confidence that allows them to create their own invented or phonic spellings, their knowledge of phonics develops naturally. As one five-year-old indicated when asked how he had managed to write some particularly difficult words:

> "I thought about the sounds in my mind then I just wrote it down."

The child was confirming what teachers believe: Writing is a phonics lesson in action. Children's involvement in the process of writing supports their phonics learning.

Writing Own Name

○ ○ ○

*C*hildren's writing in kindergarten class and beyond contains a wide variety of genres. When we explore that writing, we get an insight not only into children's thinking and their understanding of the writing process, but also their knowledge of phonics. All of that grows and extends from the child's first distinction between what is drawing and what is writing. The fish that three-year-old Dylan drew and the mark making alongside the drawing was a first obvious sign of that development, although other earlier mark making might have occurred that was less noticeable. Dylan described the five letter-like shapes that he produced as his name, and that name writing does appear to be a very important part of the exploration of print by very young children.

The importance of his or her own name to a very young child should not surprise us. After all, any preschool child at home is likely to hear his or her name used many, many times during the course of the day. Children learn that their first name is part of what makes them unique. So when observers look closely at preschool children's drawing and writing, they frequently record that own name is part of the writing. Not only the name but the drawing that children complete is often of a person and frequently is a self-portrait. The child is exploring the question, "Who am I?" and using both drawing and writing to respond to that question (figure 6–1).

At the age of three years eight months, Dylan's self-portrait was beginning to include fine features. Eyes including pupils, eyebrows, hair, mouth, and neck were all included although there was as yet no body to connect with the legs that were drawn. The writing of own name on this occasion only included four letters, rather than the five of his earlier writing, and some of those letters were disoriented. However, there was a clear <D> shape at the start of his name and there was a clear letter <l>, albeit as the last of the four letters. In between those two letters were two u-shaped letters. However, those might have been the attempt by Dylan to produce a <y> but the stalk was omitted and a letter <n> but that appeared upside down. We can never be fully certain what the child has achieved but by looking closely at what has been written and comparing that with other records of the child's writing, we get an insight into what has been attempted.

By the time he was four years and three months old, Dylan was writing his name in a very easily recognized form (figure 6–2). Of course, the letter <a> looks more like a circle on top of a stick, but it does contain the essential elements of that letter with a circle and a vertical line. Dylan had learned about the five letters of his first name and therefore about some of the letters of the written language that he would use in the coming years.

We have looked at the sequence of Dylan's name writing from his initial attempts at three years old to complete success at four years and three months with just three examples. Over that period, he wrote his name in a variety of formats on numerous occasions. In addition, the pictures that he drew frequently alongside the writing have added to the child's ability to create ever finer distinctions of

Figure 6–1. Self-portrait and own name produced by Dylan at three years eight months.

Figure 6–2. Dylan's writing of his own name at four years three months.

*Writing Own
Name*

shape. With each writing Dylan has explored the five letters of his name, their shape and orientation, and the position of each letter within his name, and he has begun to associate the sounds of his name to the letters in print. Own name writing is a self-motivated activity that contributes to a child's knowledge of letters and some sounds.

Other children at home also take time to explore their first names. In chapter 1 we saw how Alice wrote her name when she was three years and three months old. She too had shown earlier attempts to write her name. Before she was three, she too explored a variety of letter-like shapes. But at three years of age, she settled briefly upon what she called a "big A" as a means of writing her name (figure 6–3).

Within a few months of producing the "big A," Alice was consistently writing five letters with a capital *A* as the first letter. We noted when she wrote "Alioo" (shown in figure 1–3) that she was very close

Figure 6–3. Big A, Alice's way to write her name at three years.

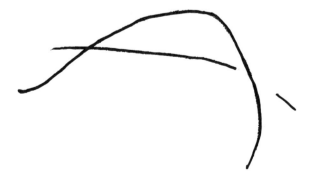

Figure 6–4. Alice's own name, written at three years four months.

to writing her own name. The two final letters may have been a problem with letter formation rather than knowledge of what needed to be written. A month later there was some confirmation of that as she wrote *Alice* with closer attempts at the letters <c> and <e> (figure 6–4).

The letter <c> still needed to be improved and the letter <e> was reversed. But it was possible to see a child working out how to write her first name in the conventional manner, and she was getting closer to accuracy week by week. By the time Alice was three years and six months old, she was consistently writing her first name accurately.

The accurate writing of her name is reflected in her drawing of a lion with a mane (figure 6–5). The detail of that drawing enables us to recognize the lion. The careful attention to detail is apparent in both the writing and the drawing. It serves as a reminder that encouraging young children to draw may be useful too as a means of being able to develop as a writer.

When we consider Dylan and Alice, we note that Alice spent less time to move from her first clear letter to the writing of her full name and she wrote her first name earlier than Dylan did. However, we would expect different rates of development from young children. Children spend six months or longer in moving from their first explorations of first name to the successful writing of it. Typically, children who have had frequent opportunities to mark make are able to write their first names sometime around their fourth birthday, although not all children do so. The writing will have been achieved without direct teaching. Of course, parents and other adults answer children's questions about own name, talk with them about it, and

Figure 6–5. Alice's own name, written at three years six months.

probably model it for them. The children hear their own names frequently and see the names of animals and people in the storybooks that are read to them. All of that supports them in writing their own name, especially if they have access to pencil and paper when they want to.

When children have achieved the writing of their first name, they have full command of those letters in their first name. But they will know far more because in a sense they have learned about the nature of literacy. They know that their own name is written

as a specific collection of letters;
along a horizontal line;
with the letters in a particular and constant sequence;
with space before and after the writing.

They do, therefore, know about the nature of literacy and the principle of how other words might be written.

They also make links from their name to other words that they see in the environment and in books. Earlier we saw that children recognize the words that they see in print that start with the same letter as the first letter in their name.

That starts with <a> just like my name.
But it's not my name.
I think it says apple.

On occasion, they move beyond the first letter of their name and comment on other letters in their name.

I've got that one in my name.

All of that tells us that the children are building knowledge of literacy as they recognize letters in an unfamiliar context as well as in the known context of their first name. Of course, at times the knowledge that the children acquire is used inappropriately for a while. Because Alice became very used to writing her name with a capital <A>, she used the <A> in other words for many months. In particular, it was some considerable time before she stopped writing *And* with the capital letter. But that was a small price to pay for the considerable learning that had developed from learning to write her first name.

Although we can talk about the importance of writing own name for most young children, some children take different routes to literacy. Prisca Martens (1996) indicates that for her daughter Sarah, writing her own name was initially not important. At around three years old Sarah wrote with invented spellings and often used just one letter for a word. But when she went to preschool at three years six months, suddenly she wanted to spell and write *Sarah* and to do so immediately. That was perhaps because name was so important in many contexts in her classroom. So within the course of one week Sarah spent a great deal of time learning to spell and then write her name. It was, her mother argues, a learned logo (66) that she used for about fifteen months. Then Sarah decided to write her name from the sounds that she heard. So after fifteen months of writing "Sarah," her name became "CAYI" and later "ZAYRI." Only later by the time she was in kindergarten was the writing of *Sarah* reestablished from her phonic knowledge and contact with print in many contexts.

However, more typically we read of the importance of own name writing in various studies of young children learning literacy at home. Marcia Baghban (1984) indicates that her daughter Giti started to write the letter <G> at about 25 months. Subsequently, she wrote <G> "on masses of paper" until by 30 months she was typically writing <G> followed by three vertical lines and some dots and dashes. The writing of four letter shapes was frequent as Giti explored her own name. In a similar way, we read of Adam becoming interested in the letter <A> at two years nine months (Schickedanz 1990) and frequently writing that letter as he developed as a writer. Subsequently, he announced as he explored letters at three years seven months, "I know a real word I can make" (Schickedanz 1990, 23).

He had written "Adam" and like the other children had learned not only to write his name but about the nature of literacy and "real words." Because we see in these examples how important name writing at home is for most children, it is clear that opportunities for exploring own name should be available in preschool and kindergarten.

Writing and using own name in the classroom

When I visited a preschool classroom, one of the four-year-old children approached me clutching a piece of paper. He then announced, "I can write my own name I can."

On the piece of paper were the three letters written in sequence to produce his name, Sam. Either from visual memory of the three letters or using phonological knowledge, he had learned to write his name and to do so with a sense of achievement. Just as Dylan, Alice, Sarah, Giti, and Adam had been when writing at home, so Sam was in the preschool interested in finding out about how his name was written.

The adults in the preschools encourage name writing in a variety of activities. Most frequently and simply they encourage the children to write their name on drawings and paintings. That serves a practical purpose of knowing whom the work belongs to as well as encouraging the children to think about literacy. When the child cannot yet write sufficiently well to distinguish it as his or her name, then the adult can write it on the artwork to indicate the owner as well as to serve as a model for the child. Both at home and in the classroom, the adults should accept the variety of writing produced by the children to signify their names. It is part of the process that leads to an accurate writing of their names.

As part of the preschool and kindergarten experience, it is useful to present numerous opportunities for the children to recognize their names. In many classrooms a collection of name cards are placed on a table for the children to select their names and then put them into a mailbox. Instead of a mailbox, a tree with hooks allows the children to hang their names like apples on a tree. The teacher can also use nametags at other times in the day to encourage the children to look carefully for their names.

We can use the children's interest in own name to link to the names of other children. The class names can be displayed in a variety of ways, particularly when children reach kindergarten. A birthday chart to show the month of birth of each child in the class serves to bring together two very important features for a young child, name and birthday. The chart then serves as a focus to talk about the names of the children with a birthday in any given month, as well as encouraging an oral awareness of the sequence of months in a year. An alphabet chart of names is also useful as a means of providing a focus. It shows the children who share the same first letter in their names. The teacher can use the chart at times to discuss with the children other letters within the name that are shared. In effect, a word wall is constructed that shows the letters of the alphabet and the children's names. The names of key characters from well-loved picture books can be used to fill spaces, maintain the interest in the chart, and provide a focus for all the letters of the alphabet.

A similar but useful activity is for the class to construct an alphabet book. Every child in the class produces a self-portrait together with the writing of his or her name. Those are then stuck into a large book in alphabetical order. When that is placed in the classroom literacy center, it often becomes a very popular book that the children want to look through. And it teaches letters of the alphabet and the alphabet sequence.

We want children to move beyond recognizing their name to writing it. So writing their name on artwork but also at other times is important. At the writing center, the children can be encouraged to write their names on lists, notes, and other writing to help the teacher. Some classrooms have a sign-in list. The children write their names on the class list at the start of the day to indicate they are present. Over time that gives a good indication of the progress being made by the children as writers. The name can be used in other ways too; for example, clapping the syllables of the first name as a group or class activity leads the children toward thinking about syllables, onset, and rime.

So we have spent the whole of this chapter thinking about just one word—the first name of the child. But it is a word of considerable importance and motivation for the child. That is emphasized in figure 6–6, which shows four-year-old Amy's (in preschool) self-por-

Figure 6–6. Amy's name and self-portrait, written and drawn at four years old.

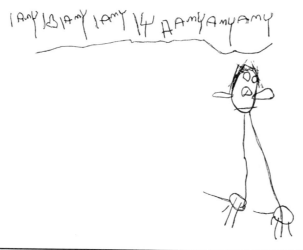

trait and some added writing (Campbell 1996, 13). We can see that Amy wrote her name six times along with a few other letters and letter-like shapes.

Amy's name was a source of literacy and phonics learning for her. Once children have the knowledge to write their names, they know how to write "a real word." They have an understanding of what it is to write a word. So they have a bridge to literacy (Davies 1988) from a word they know to many other words. Many children come to school with some additional knowledge of letters and sounds to help toward attempting those other words. No wonder then that teachers in preschool and kindergarten support children to write their names and then use the collection of names in the class to talk about words, letters, and sounds.

Using Environmental Print

○ ○ ○

*V*ery young children "read" the environment as part of coming to understand the world outside the home as well as inside. They learn about roads and sidewalks, houses and shops, grass and trees, and so forth. Their reading and understanding of the environment extends also to the more specific signs, logos, and print. They learn about that environmental print through opportunities they have to explore the outside world, observations they make of the environment, and discussion with adults about what they see. We know from a variety of sources that children learn about the print in the environment before they start preschool or school. Indeed, there is evidence of children responding to environmental print before they are two years old and substantially so after that time.

Currently, in Western societies, one of the first signs that appears to be recognized by many young children is the sign and logo for McDonald's. The logo is also a letter, so from a very early age many children are recognizing the letter <M>, although they are supported in that learning by the yellow and red coloring and the context in which they see the logo/letter. When Zachary was just fifteen months old he demonstrated a familiarity with that logo (Laminack 1991, 16), and Giti consistently identified the yellow <M> in at least three contexts: as a stand-alone item, on a billboard, and on a cup (Baghban 1984, 29). Likewise, Alice recognized the golden arches' <M> and did so outside her usual domain. On a car journey when she was two years and six months old, she noted a McDonald's in an area that she had not previously visited:

ALICE   McDonald's.

GRANDFATHER	It is McDonald's.
	What do you get there?
ALICE	Chips and a hamburger.
GRANDFATHER	Mm. Anything else?
ALICE	Pancakes.
GRANDFATHER	What about to drink?
ALICE	Milkshakes.

(Campbell 1999, 53)

Alice was able to recognize the <M> and to talk about what it was possible to purchase in McDonald's, so she was aware that the symbol represents a constant product.

Prisca Martens reports that Sarah, too, was recognizing the McDonald's <M>, along with a number of other logos such as K-Mart, Target, and STOP, by the time she was two and a half (Martens 1996, 19–20). Children recognize a variety of print in the environment. That recognition becomes increasingly sophisticated as the children experience and talk about what they see. For instance, when Caitlin was three years old she demonstrated that skill on a visit to a supermarket. As we might expect of young children, she fluctuated from wanting to push the shopping cart, to wandering around carrying a packet of tissues, to collecting an item from the shelves. On two occasions she ventured down an aisle to collect items, first a bottle of cola and then a box of corn flakes. She was successful with both of those ventures. However, it is useful to reflect on the nature of the task for a three-year-old. The shelves of cereal held a very wide variety, yet the three-year-old was able to make an accurate selection of corn flakes and a particular brand unaided. Caitlin used the colors, pictures, logo, and perhaps print to help her make the accurate choice. Nevertheless, to be successful she had to read that wealth of information and look at the fine detail. Looking at fine detail would be useful later when dealing with literacy and phonics.

Young children describe products initially for function (food or eat) and later as a category (cereal); with opportunities and experience, they become very specific (corn flakes or even the particular brand), as Harste, Woodward, and Burke (1984) describe. That behavior informs us that the children are becoming more sophisticated in their reading of environmental print, and they can do so in novel contexts. For instance, when Alice was two years ten months old, without her knowledge a flexible tape measure had been acquired to measure her head for a bicycle helmet. As she was being measured she said: "Look, TOYS 'R' US."

The measure had come from that shop and had the name written on the tape. What Alice was doing, however, was reading the logo at home rather than at the shop, and it written in blue on a yellow background rather than its usual multicolored logo. Perhaps it was the central reversed letter <R> that enabled her to read the logo/print. Whatever the case, Alice demonstrated her developing attention to print.

There are many sources of print in the environment. Children note far more than just the products and retail outlets of various kinds that we have considered. Street signs and route directions are encountered on any journey, as are large billboards. Other means of transport provide other print for children. Linda Miller (1998) indicates that her three-and-a-half-year-old daughter noted the safety instructions on the back of seats of an airplane and asked, "Does that say mummy's seat, daddy's seat, girl's seat, lady's seat, man's seat?" (Miller 1998, 104)

Young children notice print all around them and are interested in finding out what it says. Not only is it all around them, they also wear print. The writing on some T-shirts is very prominent, and they and other clothing have smaller labels as well that children are curious to explore.

In figure 7–1, not only is two-year-old Dylan wearing a T-shirt with very prominent print, he is also engaged with a storybook. He is looking at print, very clearly pointing to some fine detail of the book, and wearing print. He is surrounded by print and, we might guess, attempting to make sense of the print world in which he lives.

Children are interested in environmental print and are motivated to find out what it signals. As they explore the print, they use the color and logo to help them understand what they see. Increasingly they look at words and letters as well and talk about them with adults. When a child sees the <M> in *McDonald's* and in *K-Mart*, they notice the <M> in two contexts and hear an /M/ sound in addition to seeing the letter. Similar learning occurs with other letters from the vast amount of environmental print that they encounter. They are learning letters and sounds and doing so naturally. Because children have such an interest in environmental print and, therefore, in words and letters, it is easy to see why teachers want to replicate such experiences in the classroom to support literacy learning.

Figure 7–1. T-shirt with large print on it.

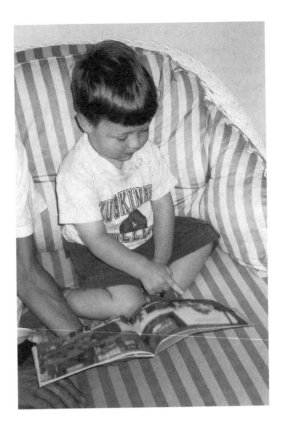

Using environmental print in the classroom

We saw in chapter 5 that when a corner of the classroom is set aside as a sociodramatic play area, it might be transformed into a post office to create numerous opportunities for writing. The area can also be transformed into a supermarket. Then environmental print becomes a major feature as numerous packages are put on display. The children can assist in setting out the display so that the cereal boxes are together and soap powders are together and on different shelves, and so forth. When they engage in imaginative play, the children will read the packets as they shop and talk about them with others as they purchase their items at the check out.

In preschool and kindergarten classrooms some of that environmental print packaging can be used to make a collection of labels to display as an alphabetical word wall or an "I can read" chart. Thus, letters and alphabetical sequence become part of the activity. In addition, a similar collection of packets can be used to construct an environmental alphabet book.

When one kindergarten class constructed an alphabet book, the children cut and stuck into the book bits of the packages. On each page they put a drawing and writing of another object beginning with the same letter. The teacher provided the heading, as shown by figure 7–2 where a capital <C> as well as a lowercase <c> are printed clearly at the top of the page. During the construction of the book, there was a lot of talk about the objects and each letter. Subsequently, this alphabet book that included environmental print was added to the literacy center. Once again, because the children had authored the book, it was inevitably a very popular book that the children were frequently using in the literacy center.

Another link between environmental print and the classroom can occur when the teacher suggests a T-shirt party. Quite simply, the children are invited to wear a T-shirt to school that has print on it. Asking the children to report to the class about the print on their T-shirt can extend the event. Then the teacher can organize activities around the T-shirts, looking for particular letters, playing "I Spy" linked to the T-shirts, attempting to create an alphabet from the cloth-

Figure 7–2. Environment alphabet book.

ing, seeking out similar letters, and getting the children to draw and write about their T-shirts. Because the children own the T-shirt print, they are typically very enthusiastic about exploring that print and therefore the words, letters, and sounds.

Young children usually understand road signs and directions when they start school. Use can be made of that knowledge in the classroom if the teacher prepares some signs and talks with the children about them. STOP is an important word for road safety and the children can be reminded about it. Then the /st/ digraph and /op/ rime unit can be used to create lists of other words that the children might know. So road safety and literacy learning are brought together as part of the classroom events. The children can also make their own signs such as "no talking" or "silence" to be placed in the literacy center; thus, the road signs are transformed into classroom signs.

A teacher might create a subject web, such as in figure 7–3, so that some of the possibilities for the classroom are recorded. Perhaps not all of the books or activities in the web will be used, and other books and activities might be suggested, but the web does remind the teacher of possible developments. In this instance, the Dr. Seuss (1963) book *Hop on Pop* not only includes *Stop* but also, as in the title, makes use of other rime /op/ words to create a rhyming text, so it is especially useful for this theme. Creative teachers are continually looking for ways to link the interests of the children to meaningful learning. Environmental print can do that in a number of ways.

Going for a print walk to select some particular environmental print is another useful activity. A usual reaction when print is looked for in the environment is just how much there is to find and discuss. This activity can be used with older classes to develop as an extended topic. For instance, a simple piece of print is found on car number plates, and that can lead to a wide range of talk, inquiry, further reading, and writing. And that is only a relatively small fraction of the print to be found outside the classroom.

Bringing environmental print into the classroom makes a good deal of sense because it links the print that the children are familiar with to classroom literacy activities. As we have seen, the teacher can use that print to consider words and talk about letters and sounds. The teacher then can extend the interest in environmental print to cover other important classroom print.

Figure 7–3. A subject web for STOP.

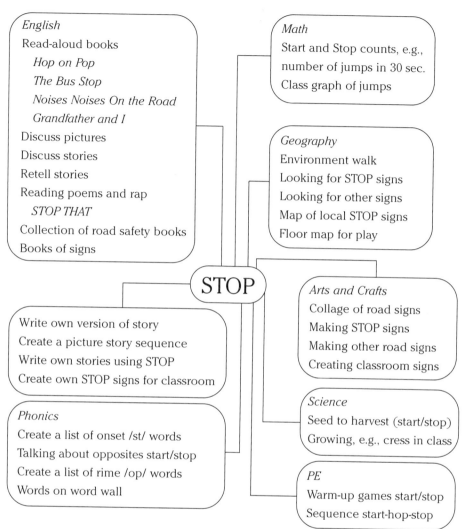

Books

Buckley, H., and J. Ormerod, 1994. *Grandfather and I.* New York: Viking Puffin.

Hellen, N. 1988. *The Bus Stop.* London: Arum Books for Children.

Seuss, Dr. 1963. *Hop on Pop.* New York: Beginner Books, Random House.

Simeon, L., and R. Clifford, 1994. *STOP THAT.* New York: Penguin.

Wells, T. 1988. *Noises Noises on the Road.* London: Walker Books.

Creating Classroom Print

○ ○ ○

*I*n the previous chapter we looked at print in the environment and the way in which children respond to that print before entering school. Then we considered how that print might be used in the classroom. Now we look at the variety of print that many children meet in the home and note how a print-rich home supports a child's literacy learning. With that in mind, we look too at the importance of taking that idea into the classroom and creating a print-rich classroom. Of course, it is important too that the abundance of classroom print is discussed on a regular basis. But first we need to look at the print in the home.

Print in the home

One of the print features that is often noted in homes is some form of alphabet chart. It is typically brightly colored and has the alphabet with an object against each letter, for example, <Aa> apple. Of course, learning print features requires more than just having an alphabet on display. It needs to be talked about with the child. Alice had an alphabet chart among the colorful posters in her bedroom. When her parents talked with her about the chart, she would talk about the object or name the letter. When she was not yet two years old, it was most likely to be comments about the objects, so at one year eight months a typical conversation was:

FATHER   <T> is for?

ALICE   Aah. (*Cuddles an imaginary teddy bear*)

FATHER   <U> is for?

ALICE   (*Holds out hand to check for rain—umbrella*)

FATHER   And the <V> is for?

ALICE   Brm brm (*van*)

FATHER   <W> is for the?

ALICE   (*Holds up her hand and looks at her wrist—the object in the picture being a wristwatch*)

(Campbell 1999, 31)

Alice was involved in the discussion and heard the letters being named. It is very likely that knowledge of letter names and letter shapes was being developed, although that was not the object of the father and daughter game.

Parents do not have to purchase an alphabet chart to get print into the home. Print arrives in many ways. An instructional manual accompanies the purchase of an electronic item. Young children see adults trying to make sense of those instructions. Letters and junk mail arrive in most homes frequently and young children are inquisitive about that mail and learn from it. Sometimes forms arrive in the mail that the adult has to complete. On those occasions, young children not only see print but may also witness a model of writing as the form is completed. At other times, greeting cards of some kind arrive in the mail. Recall that we saw in chapter 1 that Alice had learned about the nature of birthday greetings. She used that learning to construct her short birthday greetings "to Gd" (figure 1–2). Children learn from the variety of print at home and that includes newspapers, magazines, and books that might be brought into the home. Occasionally, the TV schedule in a newspaper is a strong motivation for reading for three- and four-year-old children. But the television can be a source of reading in other ways.

The commercials shown on television may support children's reading. Jane Torrey (1969) reports that John, the third of five children, appeared to have learned to read before going to school from television commercials. She reminds us that those commercials are repeated frequently, they are designed to get our attention, and they are usually loud, lively, and simple. The frequent repetition means that if children do not learn the rhymes and such on the first occasion, there will be many subsequent showings to learn the rhymes and read the words. John learned the commercials and could recite them as they appeared on the screen. So he knew the words and was able to relate those words to the print on the screen. The earliest evidence of that knowledge being carried forward was when he demonstrated an ability to read the labels on cans in the kitchen. Jane Torrey concludes that "from commercials a child could get a start on a basic vocabulary and make a few inferences about phonics (and) extend his reading knowledge through phonics" (150). John learned phonics naturally from engagement with the print in the home.

There are so many ways that print in the home might support children's literacy learning that we do not always notice the examples. Children are inquisitive and that includes wanting to know about print. When Alice was three years six months old, she inquired about a book, a road atlas, that was being read:

ALICE   What's that?

GRANDFATHER   A book.

ALICE   It's not a reading book.

GRANDFATHER   Isn't it? What is it then?

ALICE   (*Pause*)

GRANDFATHER   What book is it?

ALICE   It's a which-way-you're-going book.

(Campbell 1999, 81)

Alice's description of the road atlas was sensible since she lacked the experience of using and talking about such books. However, it does show us again how young children are naturally interested in print and in this case reading and understanding that the fine detail in this book shows "which way you're going."

Of course, the print that children meet at home varies, and different cultures emphasize particular forms of print. But children meet print in some form or other at home and learn from it. For example, by the time she was five years old, Alice had seen recipes being used in the kitchen. So she decided that she would write her own recipe for a "shepherd's pie" (figure 8–1).

Alice had learned quite a bit about literacy and phonics without the direct teaching that occurs at school. First, it was apparent that she had learned about the format for presenting a recipe. The recipe is set out as would be expected in a recipe book. Then there are four of the frequently used key words—*to, a, of, and*—in this writing and they were written in a conventional manner. The remainder of the writing includes four numerals—6, 7, 1, 0—and some words that demonstrate Alice's knowledge of letters and sounds. Those words are:

pie	piy
shepherd's	sepas
grams	gras (gas)
onion	uyn
potatoes	ptatos
beans	biass
cheese	cess

What phonics has this five-year-old learned naturally from a wide and varied engagement with print? At the simplest level of analysis, we can see the seven words of invented/phonic spellings all have an appropriate first letter. Although *onion* is not spelled with the beginning letter <o>, nevertheless, the five-year-old's attempt at this word is very interesting. It is evident that she has listened to the sounds of the word and then represented them on paper in a way that makes sense. With more experience of words and after seeing the

Figure 8–1. Alice's recipe for shepherd's pie, written at five years old.

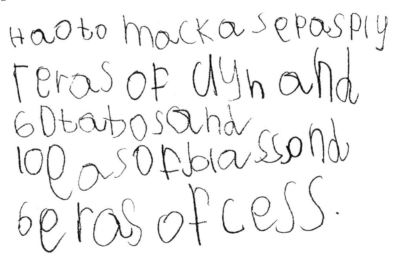

word *onion* in conventional spelling, it is likely that she will quickly adjust to that convention. We can also note that the sound of the last letter is apparent in each word. There are also vowels in place, although not always the correct vowel, in each of the spellings.

The opportunity to write in the genre of recipe encouraged Alice to write and to think about phonics as she did so. This is merely one example of home print providing a source for literacy learning and reminding us that we need to replicate such learning in the classroom. Classroom print is an important support for children's literacy and phonic learning. It needs to be provided and discussed in the classroom with young children.

Using classroom print

The print that young children experience at home is being used for real purposes. Letters, greeting cards, junk mail, forms, instructions, newspapers, magazines and books, TV schedules, TV commercials, food labels, road atlases, and recipes all have a purpose, and both adults and children respond to that print. The alphabet chart doesn't convey a message but often it is part of the colorful decoration in a child's bedroom, as well as being a source of print and introduction to letters. How can classroom print be provided to serve a similarly useful purpose?

Earlier we noted that in the preschool and kindergarten classrooms, an area is often set aside for imaginative or sociodramatic play. Organized as a supermarket, post office, travel agency, veterinarian's office, restaurant, newspaper office, gas station, or garage, it provides considerable scope for the adult to provide print that is linked to the setup and highly appropriate. Recall that the print that is provided can then lead to the children drawing and writing. The adults in the classroom can also use the print to talk about names and words. For instance, when the area is used as a veterinarian's office, there might be a number of bold pictures of animals with their names alongside. Those can be used briefly to talk about the name and perhaps link the first letter to first letters of the names of the children. Each play setting provides the scope for different print to be included for a real purpose.

There is other print in the classroom that serves a real purpose. Many teachers include clear labels to indicate the drawer for pencils, crayons, plain paper, and so on. Additionally, there are classroom signs. In the literacy center, we recognized that there might be notices to indicate "only six children in the literacy center at one time please." There might also be brief notices with other rules such as "Do not disturb the children reading." The rules can be displayed with the same features and colors of a road sign. Those signs are very clear and bold with just the important two, three, or four words; not only does it give a clear message, it also reminds the children about road signs, which can be the source of another discussion. Lengthier signs might tell about the lending system or be a roster for keeping the center tidy. Then particular books can be displayed and a short notice can tell "about this book." Likewise, there can be displays such as books about bears, and the bear is a popular subject of many picture books. A collection of books by a particular author can be displayed, too. With each display, a brief bold notice in large print can be useful to tell the children about the subject. Of course, it is insufficient to just provide the notice; it has to be read to and with the children and then talked about from time to time. Thus, the notices become the focus for a shared reading where meaning is conveyed and words and letters are considered.

With very young children, the alphabet is an important part of the classroom print and it can be provided in a number of ways. We have looked at how one class had an environmental alphabet book that was constructed as a class effort. Also, we considered the usefulness of having alphabet books in the literacy center. Alphabet books made by the children can be added to that collection.

Figure 8–2 shows part of an alphabet book created by one first-grade child; we can see the <E> and <F> page. For those two letters, the child drew and named an elephant and a flower. *Flower* was spelled conventionally; however, there was also the invented spelling of "elefght." It may be unconventional, but we can deduce how it might have been formed. The first two syllables are correct with /el/ and /e/, but /phant/ presented difficulties. First, the /f/ for /ph/ was a sensible choice based on the sound. The /ght/ is more problematic but at that stage the first grader may have been recalling a visual memory of some words such as *night, right, might,* and *sight* and relating that to the word *elephant.* Whatever were the rules being generated, it does show a young child working hard with letters and sounds in order to make sense in writing.

When all the children had completed their books, a collection of alphabet books was added to a small box in the literacy center. Because the children had authored the books, they were of great

Figure 8–2. One page of an alphabet book created by a first-grade child.

interest and frequently looked at by them. Occasionally, the teacher selected one of the alphabet books to talk about a letter and remind the children about the object drawn and named on the page and to ask for other possibilities. At that time, for instance, *elephant* can be written in large print along with other <e> examples so that the children see a model of the spelling of *elephant* and other <e> words. Creating their own alphabet books teaches letters and the alphabet sequence and the writing encourages the children to think of letters, sounds, and as we have just seen, letter clusters.

An alphabetical word wall is an important part of the print in the classroom. Teachers in preschool and K–2 classrooms select an area of classroom wall for this activity. It is very important that the word wall be positioned at such a height that the children can see it easily. Then a space is designated for each letter of the alphabet, either by using bold marker pens on large sheets of paper or by using color tape to mark the boxes for each letter. For the youngest children, a good starting point is to have the first names of children placed on the word wall. It is best to do that as part of a shared activity. As Cunningham and Allington (1998) argue, it is not enough to have a word wall; the teacher must *do* a word wall. As a starting point with young children, the teacher can talk about where to place, for instance, "Adam" and "Alice" names on the wall and to ask if any other names belong in the <Aa> box. During the discussion, the first names of all the children are written into a box for the correct letters. Inevitably, because it is about their names, children are interested. And it allows for comparisons to be made about the first letters of names. It can also extend to looking for other letters within names that are similar. Letters and alphabet sequence are learned naturally as part of the discussion because they are central to the talk of the children and teacher.

With the youngest children, adding names of loved characters from read-alouds can be a useful way of filling in empty letters and of making comparisons with their own names. The teacher has a number of options for adding further words. Key words might be added, perhaps in a different bold color so that they stand out. Or interesting words that the children meet in their reading and writing can be added. Of course, words need to be taken away as well. Too many words on the word wall make them less easy to read.

Margaret Moustafa (1997) has a simple strategy to make changing the words on the word wall easy. She suggests securing a plastic shower curtain liner to the classroom wall with an area for each letter of the alphabet clearly shown. The words to be placed on the wall are written on small strips of card. Then they are attached to the liner using "transparent tape placed horizontally on the upper edge of the paper" (93). That system helps the teacher to adjust the word wall very quickly. For instance, the teacher might decide to add /st/ words in the <Ss> box with *stop*. So with all the other <s> words removed, the suggestions from the children of (*sty, stand, step,* etc.) can be added to the wall. Moustafa also suggests occasionally emphasizing rime units rather than onsets. Now in the <Aa> box there might be *and* but also *band, sand,* and *stand* so that the rime unit of *-and* is presented, seen, and talked about. To emphasize that element for the children, the *-and* rime unit can be written in a different bold color.

Whatever the teacher decides, it is important to recall that in addition to providing the word wall, the teacher needs to *do* the word wall. Words need to be talked about. The teacher need only make a brief comment about one of the letters or rime units during the course of the day for the children to be reminded of the words, letters, sounds, and rimes on the wall. When that takes place the children use the word wall for their own purposes at other times of the day. So letters, sounds, rimes, and words are thought about frequently.

Classroom Activities to Promote Phonic Learning

○ ○ ○

*T*hroughout the book there are suggestions of classroom activities to promote phonic learning. Here those are brought together as a bulleted list of ideas for teachers to use. The lists are provided under the four headings of letter/alphabet knowledge, phonemic awareness, onset and rime, and letter-sound relationships. Of course, an activity can often promote phonic learning across those boundaries. However, busy teachers may find that these four lists support their classroom teaching.

Letter/alphabet knowledge

We know that many children start school already with a secure knowledge of letters and perhaps the alphabet. They do so because they have made marks, engaged with reading and writing, and talked about literacy with at least one adult. All of the suggested classroom activities are natural extensions of those literacy events at home. For children who have reached school without those initial experiences, the classroom activities provide a base of interesting literacy events for learning about letters.

- Provide opportunities for young children to mark make.
- Ensure that children draw and write daily.
- Talk with children about their writing, words, and letters.
- Encourage the children to write their own names.

- Establish a birthday chart to show each child's month of birth and name.
- Create an alphabet chart or word wall with the children's names.
- Use the children's first names to compare first and other letters.
- Add the names of well-loved characters from picture books to the alphabet chart.
- Create an alphabet book of class names and self-portraits for the literacy center.
- Arrange an alphabet environmental print display.
- Construct an alphabet book using environmental print.
- Organize a T-shirt party to look at words, first letters, and the alphabet sequence.
- Use road signs to consider the link between road safety and literacy.
- Develop classroom print of labels and signs that have a purpose and provide words to be discussed.
- Support children in the writing of their own alphabet books.
- Create other alphabet books: for example, an animal alphabet book.
- Sing the alphabet song to provide a reminder of letter names and the sequence of the letters.
- Use the word wall to talk about words, letters, and sounds.
- Provide regular shared readings of big print so that the print can be seen, shared, and discussed.
- After a shared reading with big print, choose a word to talk about the first letter of the word, the letter name, and its most usual sound.
- Draw attention to a key word after a shared reading to help children add the word to visual memory.
- Have the children compare the first letter of a character from a shared reading story with names in the classroom.

- Include literacy materials in the corner set aside for sociodramatic play to encourage the children to mark make and write.

- Develop a writing center to extend the opportunities for writing.

- Encourage the children to write the first letter of a word as they share the pen during interactive writing.

- Provide a variety of opportunities to draw, mark make, and write after a read-aloud.

Phonemic awareness

When children are given daily opportunities to play with language by singing, writing, and engaging with read-alouds, they develop an awareness of sounds. That awareness becomes more acute over time and the children develop an awareness of phonemes in words. Typically, they recognize the initial and then the final phoneme in words before they become aware of phonemes within words as their experiences with literacy are extended.

- Provide shared writing and shared reading of nursery rhymes, poems, songs, and rap.

- Learn nursery rhymes, poems, songs, and rap as a regular part of each day.

- Play letter games such as "I Spy" to think about letters and sounds and attempt to deduce the initial phoneme in a word.

- Create a list of words of objects in the classroom that begin with a particular letter.

- Compare and contrast all the first and then all the last letters of the children's first names.

- Isolate a sound and think creatively about it (e.g., when the children considered /sn/ and redesigned a new title and cover for *Sniff-Snuff-Snap*).

- Read aloud poetry, alphabet books, and stories that contain alliteration.

- Encourage the children to write short alliterations.

· Encourage young children to write; it requires them to attempt
to isolate, identify, and use the phonemes for invented
spellings in some of the words they are attempting to write.

Onset and rime

As we have seen in many of the examples in this book, young children enjoy playing with rhymes and making up rhymes. When some
of the stories that are read aloud to them contain rhymes, it creates
an extra interest. From that variety of rhymes, and with the support
of an adult, the children quickly learn about onset and rime and syllables, and that is a substantial basis for learning more widely about
other aspects of phonics.

· Read aloud picture books with good stories including
some with onset and rime.

· Pause during readings to allow time for the children
to contribute a rhyming word.

· Read aloud poetry that will give further insights into
the use of onset and rime.

· Play language games such as "I'm Thinking of a Word"
to emphasize onset and rime and to suggest working
out a word by analogy.

· Sing frequently to engage with onset and rime elements
of language.

· Help the children to clap the syllables in their own first name
and the syllables in the rhymes and songs.

· Use time after a shared reading to draw attention
to onset and rime units.

· Encourage the children to provide other words to rhyme with
the rime or phonogram from the shared reading.

· Create a list of rhyming words that are provided
by the children.

· Adapt the word wall to move words with ease and
highlight rime units.

· Use shared writing to talk with the children about
rhyming words in nursery rhymes and songs.

- Encourage the children to write some of the rhyming words when sharing the pen during interactive writing.
- Encourage children to write stories with simple rhyme structures.

Letter-sound relationships

When children have knowledge of letters and alphabet, a developing phonemic awareness, and a familiarity with onset and rime, they develop an ever more sophisticated use of letter-sound relationships. That sophistication is extended as they read, write, and talk with their teachers about language daily.

- Play language games (e.g., "Hangman") that involve a good deal of thinking about letters, sounds, and spellings.
- Use read-alouds as the basis for the children to draw and write.
- Follow a shared reading by looking at key words, picking out prefixes and suffixes, and talking about the spelling of complex words.
- Use part of guided reading sessions to consider letters and sounds.
- Provide opportunities for independent reading.
- Use individual reading conferences and other classroom observation to develop a picture of the child's letter and sound knowledge.
- Use shared writing to talk with the children about some letter-sound relationships.
- Create mini-lessons on aspects of phonics (such as the *-ing* words we noted) based on what the children are writing or reading.
- Support children during the process of writing as they produce invented or phonic spellings where they have to consider letter-sound relationships.
- Provide opportunities for the children to write haiku poetry as a creative activity that requires them to manipulate syllables.

- Take a "print walk" to use some print as the basis for an inquiry.

- Use other subject areas across the curriculum to provide numerous opportunities for writing.

- Organize class projects, individual topics, and one-day themes to extend the children's thinking and to provide authentic reasons for writing.

All That Phonics Learning

○ ○ ○

I argue in this book that children will gain letter knowledge and know the alphabet, develop phonological and phonemic awareness, learn about onset and rime (and therefore syllables), and develop increasingly sophisticated knowledge of letter-sound relationships from engagement in worthwhile writing and reading activities that they also talk about. Teachers can ensure that such phonic learning takes place without its being a dominant feature of the teaching within the classroom. Rather, it develops naturally out of the writing, especially when invented or phonic spelling is encouraged and when reading activities are supported and encouraged by the teacher.

By looking first at three very young children learning literacy at home without direct teaching, we noted how they began to read, write, and use phonics. Many of the opportunities and experiences that occurred for those children are also provided in the classroom for young children. Of course, with a classroom of children, the activities and events change somewhat. However, it is still possible to provide reading and writing that are for real purposes and make sense to the children. From that, the children also learn phonics.

We discussed how a grade 1 class enjoyed a read-aloud of the *Hairy Maclary from Donaldson's Dairy* (Dodd 1983) story and how some of the children wrote about the dogs. Earlier we noted that in a grade 2 class, the children wrote rhyming stories of their own. Here the younger children had the benefit of hearing the story and getting a sense of the onset and rime features, before each child wrote a more simple sentence as a response.

Figure 10–1. A child's response to a reading of *Hairy Maclary from Donaldson's Dairy.*

hermalcry is a sluf gy dog and he went for a worsy with his frens and Theay scarud in The dusbin

As figure 10–1 shows, one child wrote: "Hermclerey is a srufey dog and he went for a worcr with his frens and theay seatud in the dusbin." Once again we see a child producing a drawing that begins to capture some of the features of four of the dogs. The writing carries an appropriate account of one of the events in the story. That writing contains 13 conventional spellings including five key words—*a, and, in, is, the.*

is	a	dog	and	he	went	for
a	with	his	and	in	the	

So the young child is able to make good use of a visual memory of some words. There are also seven invented or phonic spellings:

Hermclerey	Hairy Maclary
srufy	scruffy
worcr	walk
frens	friends
theay	they
seatud	searched
dusbin	dustbin

Those spellings tell us of a child who has learned a good deal about the letters and sounds of English. Each of the seven words (I'm treating *Hairy Maclary* as one word here following the child's writing) has the appropriate first letter and first phoneme. The same is true for the word ending where the child has represented the sounds appropriately. Indeed, as we read what the child has written, we detect how close it is to the sounds produced with the actual words. Interestingly, I have seen "frens" written for "friends" by many children and we have seen two examples of it in this book (Sam's pig story in chapter 5 also included "frens").

But the children move on. With more opportunities for reading and writing and a teacher willing to talk about both content and language, including aspects of phonics, we can be confident of their making progress toward conventional writing. The progress occurs because, as we have seen, systematic and extensive phonics are provided naturally. They are provided within and along with real reading and writing activities to support phonic learning.

There are numerous classroom activities that support the learning of phonics which flow naturally from the reading and writing for real purposes in the classroom. There can also be minilessons that draw attention to particular phonic learning, such as the lesson on the consonant blend *sn-* that we noted. But that minilesson had a main creative element that involved the children in redesigning a book cover as well as thinking about particular words. When the children complete an activity like the *sn-* task, I think most teachers would believe that the children would have a firm base to deal with other *sn-* words. But do we then have to provide other similar activities for *sc-, sh-, sk-, sl-, sm-, sp-, sq-, st-, sw-?* Or might it be the case that once children have worked intensively in one area, there is a carryover to similar areas? Thompson's (1999) suggestion of "induced sub-lexical relations"—that the child learns "largely implicitly and hence unconsciously" (34) from experience with other aspects of letter-sound relationships—seems appropriate. Many, although not all, children understand a wider range of letter-sound relationships from dealing intensively with one feature. Of course, that does not mean that *sc-, sh-,* and so on are ignored, but we do not have to systematically and extensively deal with each consonant blend (or all other phonic elements); to do so is to suggest that children are ignorant until they are taught. It would deny that they are constructively making sense of language and literacy as they engage with it extensively at school and in many cases long before coming to school.

Children learn from a variety of sources. Experiences with reading and writing that include the teacher and children talking about aspects of language (including ideas, content, phrases, words, and letters) extend the phonic learning. As we have noted, one of the most important ways to get children to consider letters, onset and rime, letter-sound relationships, and spelling patterns is through writing. As Marilyn Jager Adams states, "Inventing spellings is essentially a process of phonics" (Adams 1990, 387). So getting children to write, write, and write some more for a real purpose on worthwhile activities is a very important means of ensuring that phonics is learned naturally on a daily basis. Additionally, when teachers constantly observe closely what the children achieve as they read and write, then knowledge of the children's phonic learning can be gained. If omissions are apparent in that phonic learning, then observant teachers develop literacy activities so that the children encounter the area within a real literacy event. But reading and writing, and a willingness to talk about letters and sounds related to that reading and writing, encourage phonics learning naturally.

eferences

Adams, M. J. 1990. *Beginning to Read: Thinking and Learning about Print.* Cambridge: MIT Press.

Baghban, M. 1984. *Our Daughter Learns to Read and Write.* Newark: International Reading Association.

Butler, D. 1998. *Babies Need Books: Sharing the Joy of Books with Children from Birth to Six.* Rev. ed. Portsmouth: Heinemann.

Campbell, R. 1996. *Literacy in Nursery Education.* Stoke-on-Trent: Trentham Books.

———. 1998. "A Three-Year-Old Learning Literacy at Home." *Early Years* 19 (1): 76–89.

———. 1999. *Literacy from Home to School: Reading with Alice.* Stoke-on-Trent: Trentham Books.

———. 2001. *Read-Alouds with Young Children.* Newark: International Reading Association.

Chukovsky, K. 1963. *From Two to Five.* Berkeley: University of California Press.

Clay, M. 1985. *The Early Detection of Reading Difficulties.* Auckland: Heinemann.

Cunningham, P., and R. Allington. 1998. *Classrooms That Work: They Can All Read and Write.* New York: Longman.

Davies, A. 1988. "Children's Names: Bridges to Literacy?" *Research in Education* 40: 19–31.

Fountas, I., and G. Pinnell. 1996. *Guided Reading: Good First Teaching for All Children.* Portsmouth: Heinemann.

Goodman, Y., D. Watson, and C. Burke. 1987. *Reading Miscue Inventory: Alternative Procedures.* New York: Richard Owen.

Graves, D. 1983. *Writing: Teachers and Children at Work.* Portsmouth: Heinemann.

Harste, J. C., V. A. Woodward, and C. L. Burke. 1984. *Language Stories & Literacy Lessons.* Portsmouth: Heinemann.

Holdaway, D. 1979. *The Foundations of Literacy.* London: Ashton Scholastic.

Johnson, P. 1995. *Children Making Books.* Reading: Reading and Language Information Centre, University of Reading.

Laminack, L. 1991. *Learning with Zachary.* Richmond Hill: Scholastic.

Martens, P. 1996. *I Already Know How to Read: A Child's View of Literacy.* Portsmouth: Heinemann.

McCarrier, A., G. Pinnell, and I. Fountas. 2000. *Interactive Writing.* Portsmouth: Heinemann.

Miller, L. 1998. "Literacy Interactions through Environmental Print." In *Facilitating Preschool Literacy,* edited by R. Campbell. Newark: International Reading Association.

Mills, H., T. O'Keefe, and D. Stephens. 1992. *Looking Closely: Exploring the Role of Phonics in One Whole Language Classroom.* Urbana: National Council of Teachers of English.

Moustafa, M. 1997. *Beyond Traditional Phonics: Research Discoveries and Reading Instruction.* Portsmouth: Heinemann.

Opitz, M. 2000. *Rhyme and Reason.* Portsmouth: Heinemann.

Pinnell, G. S., and I. Fountas. 2003. *Phonics Lessons: Letters, Words, and How They Work.* Portsmouth: Heinemann.

Rog, L. 2001. *Early Literacy Instruction in Kindergarten.* Portsmouth: Heinemann.

Routman, R. 1991. *Invitations: Changing as Teachers and Learners K–12.* Portsmouth: Heinemann.

Schickedanz, J. A. 1990. *Adam's Righting Revolutions.* Portsmouth: Heinemann.

Strickland, D. S. 1998. *Teaching Phonics Today: A Primer for Educators.* Newark: International Reading Association.

Strickland, D. S., and L. M. Morrow, eds. 1989. *Emerging Literacy: Young Children Learn to Read and Write.* Newark: International Reading Association.

Strickland, D. S., and L. M. Morrow, eds. 2000. *Beginning Reading and Writing.* Newark: International Reading Association.

Thompson, B. 1999. "The Process of Learning to Identify Words." In *Learning to Read: Beyond Phonics and Whole Language,* edited by B. Thompson and T. Nicholson. Newark: International Reading Association.

Torrey, J. 1969. "Learning to Read without a Teacher: A Case Study." In *Psycholinguistics and Reading,* edited by F. Smith. New York: Holt, Rinehart, and Winston.

Trelease, J. 1995. *The New Read-Aloud Handbook.* London: Penguin Books.

Wilde, S. 1997. *What's a Schwa Sound Anyway? A Holistic Guide to Phonetics, Phonics, and Spelling.* Portsmouth: Heinemann.

Children's Books

Atwood, M. 1995. *Princess Prunella and the Purple Peanut.* New York: Workman Publishing.

Base, G. 1986. *Animalia.* New York: Harry Abrams.

Bond, M. 1992. *Paddington at the Seaside.* London: HarperCollins.

Buckley, H., and J. Ormerod, 1994. *Grandfather and I.* New York: Viking Puffin.

Carle, E. 1969. *The Very Hungry Caterpillar.* New York: Philomel Books.

———. 1988. *Do You Want to Be My Friend?* Boston: Houghton Mifflin.

———. 1990. *The Very Quiet Cricket.* London: Hamish Hamilton.

———. 1995. *The Very Lonely Firefly.* London: Hamish Hamilton.

Dodd, L. 1983. *Hairy Maclary from Donaldson's Dairy.* Harmondsworth: Puffin Books.

———. 1990. *Slinky Malinki.* Harmondsworth: Puffin Books.

———. 1995. *Sniff-Snuff-Snap!* Harmondsworth: Puffin Books.

Goodhart, P. 1997. *Row, Row, Row Your Boat.* New York: Scholastic.

Hellen, N. 1988. *The Bus Stop.* London: Arum Books for Children.

Hutchins, P. 1972. *Good-Night Owl.* London: The Bodley Head.

Lacome, J. 1993. *Walking through the Jungle.* London: Walker Books.

Radcliffe, T. 1996. *Cimru the Seal.* London: Puffin Books.

Seuss, Dr. 1960. *Green Eggs and Ham.* New York: Beginner Books, Random House.

———. 1963. *Hop on Pop.* New York: Beginner Books, Random House.

Simeon, L., and R. Clifford. 1994. *STOP THAT.* New York: Penguin.

Wells, T. 1988. *Noises Noises on the Road.* London: Walker Books.

$\mathcal{I}$ndex

○ ○ ○